ONCE DIVIDED

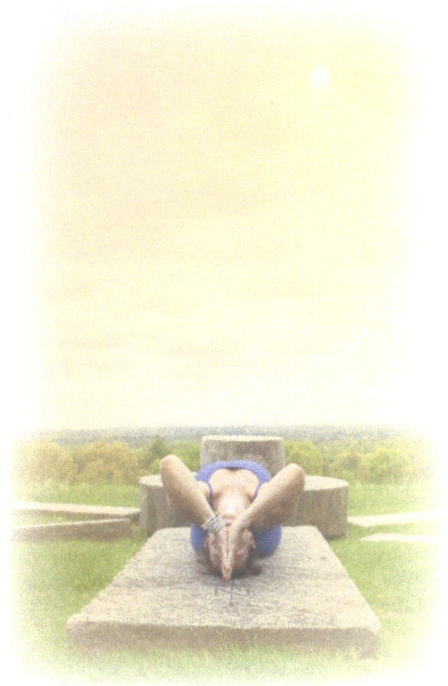

ONCE DIVIDED

WORDS AND IMAGES

SUSAN CURRIE

SHANTI ARTS PUBLISHING

BRUNSWICK, MAINE

once divided
words and images

published by shanti arts publishing
designed by shanti arts designs

shanti arts llc
193 hillside road
brunswick, maine 04011
shantiarts.com

printed in the united states of america

ISBN: 978-1-941830-85-7 (softcover)
ISBN: 978-1-941830-86-4 (digital)

library of congress control number: 2016942249

acknowledgments

"a thing fills with exactly the radiance you accord it." —lia purpura

i have of late heard his holiness the dalai lama predicting that, "the next buddha may be the sangha." i am ever grateful for the tribes who share this intention to live more fully awake and resist the mounting speed and the ruckus. i would especially like to thank joyce tenneson, tara brach, sylvia boorstein, james baraz, jack kornfield, mary grace orr, and nancy huelsburg for their ongoing teachings. and, namaste to all of the willing who step in front of my lens and bare their souls. you are truly the light. thank you also to christine cote for her interest in my work and her immense talent in weaving together this quilt. bless you jennifer allen for always having my back! to hazel, i have only you to thank for the gift of this "feeling sorry for everyone" gene. my rudder. to my parents, much love and thanks for all that you continue to do in my support. and to david, hannah and max . . . this one's for you.

traction (page 17) — includes material from the poem "ash wednesday" by t.s. eliot

the thing with feathers (page 30) — includes material from the poem "hope is the thing with feathers" by emily dickinson

scenery (pages 58-9) — includes material from "this land is your land" by woody guthrie

re *pose* (page 66) — includes material from *the way of the bodhisattva* by shantideva

holy smoke (page 72) — includes material from the hymn "keep awake, be always ready" by arthur g. clyde

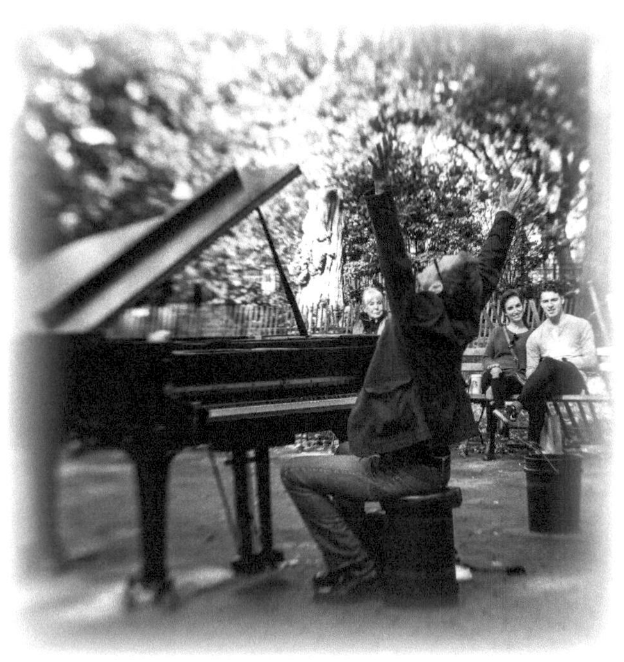

contents

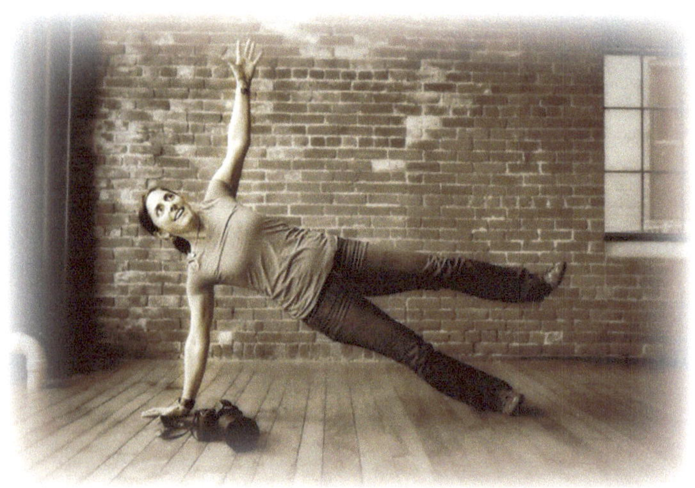

author photograph by mary ann alwan

introduction

you might say that i backed into this poetry game, my photographs serving as the bridge. i suppose i write for the same reason that i drag this camera everywhere i roam, simply to shine a light on all the glorious "meanwhiles" happening in the midst of the chatter. while some lenses point in the direction of what's trending, i tend to incline elsewhere. and, in the words of st. augustine, i document "not in order to say something, but in order to not remain altogether silent." no grand agenda. the only intention in sharing my account is to offer some room to pause, a space in which to breathe and re-set the compass.

after years of seeking, stumbling, and trying to figure it out — the words, the pictures . . . . for me it has all come down to "the radiance you accord". attention. the missing link ever before me. i didn't unearth this simple truth in books or in darkrooms. rather, my epiphanies began quietly, over time, through the prayer poses of yoga and by spending as much time as possible in the great outdoors. in these two practices doorways appeared — one seamlessly into the other, over time. the path never demanded that i renounce anything, sit perfectly still on a cushion, or master any intricate physical postures. the only requirement, my attention.

waking up to life . . . all are welcome. and, it is never too late to begin. truly. perhaps in these pages you will find prompts for stillness or creativity or prayer. and, as any artist would advise, please don't allow me the last say in the matter. in these pages, i invite you to continue on with your own thinking. use the white space found among my words and images to gather, to wonder, and to maybe unlatch some doors all your own. nothing to figure out. simply let your heart and soul be your pilot. there's not so much to it if you're in.

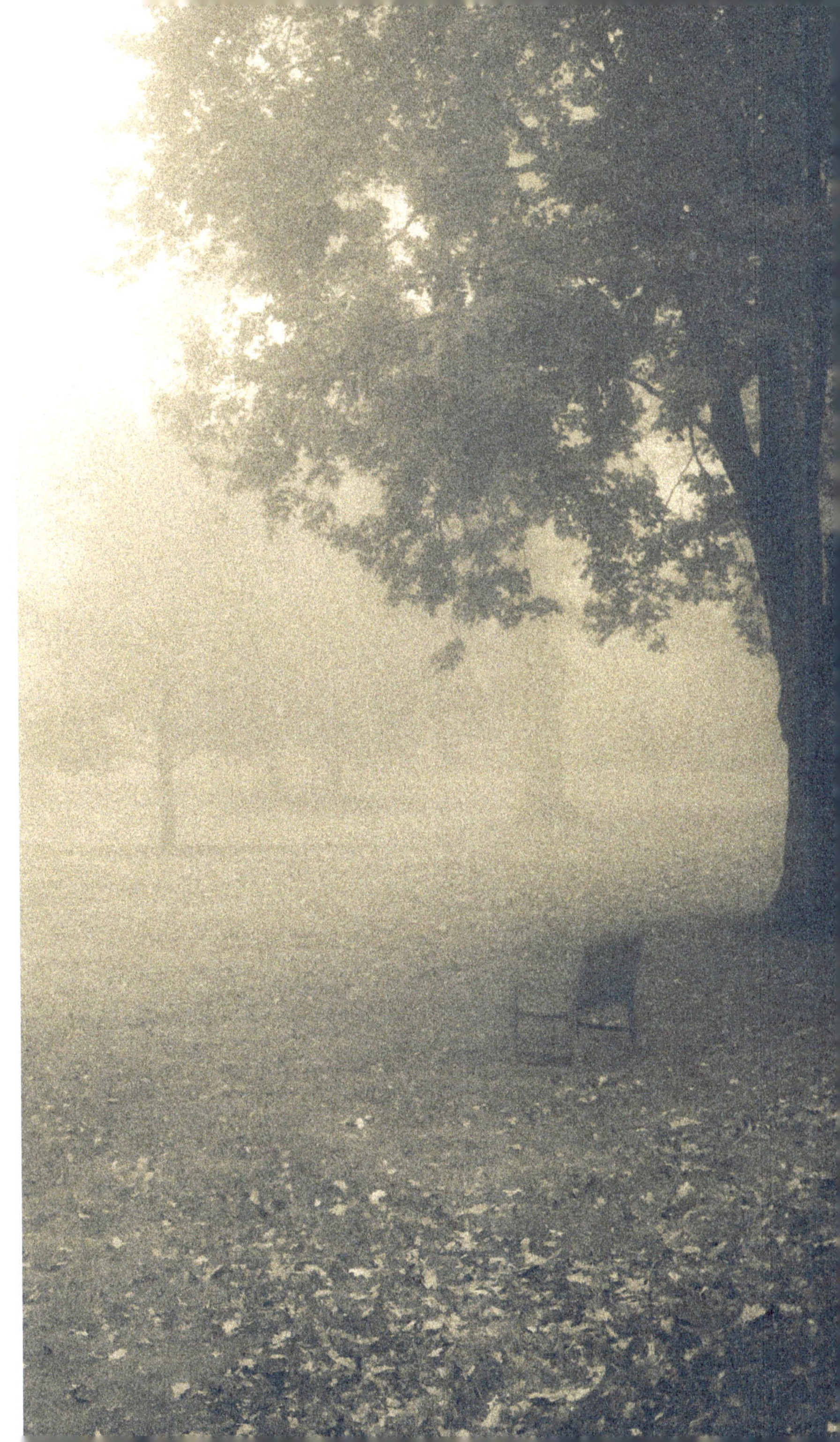

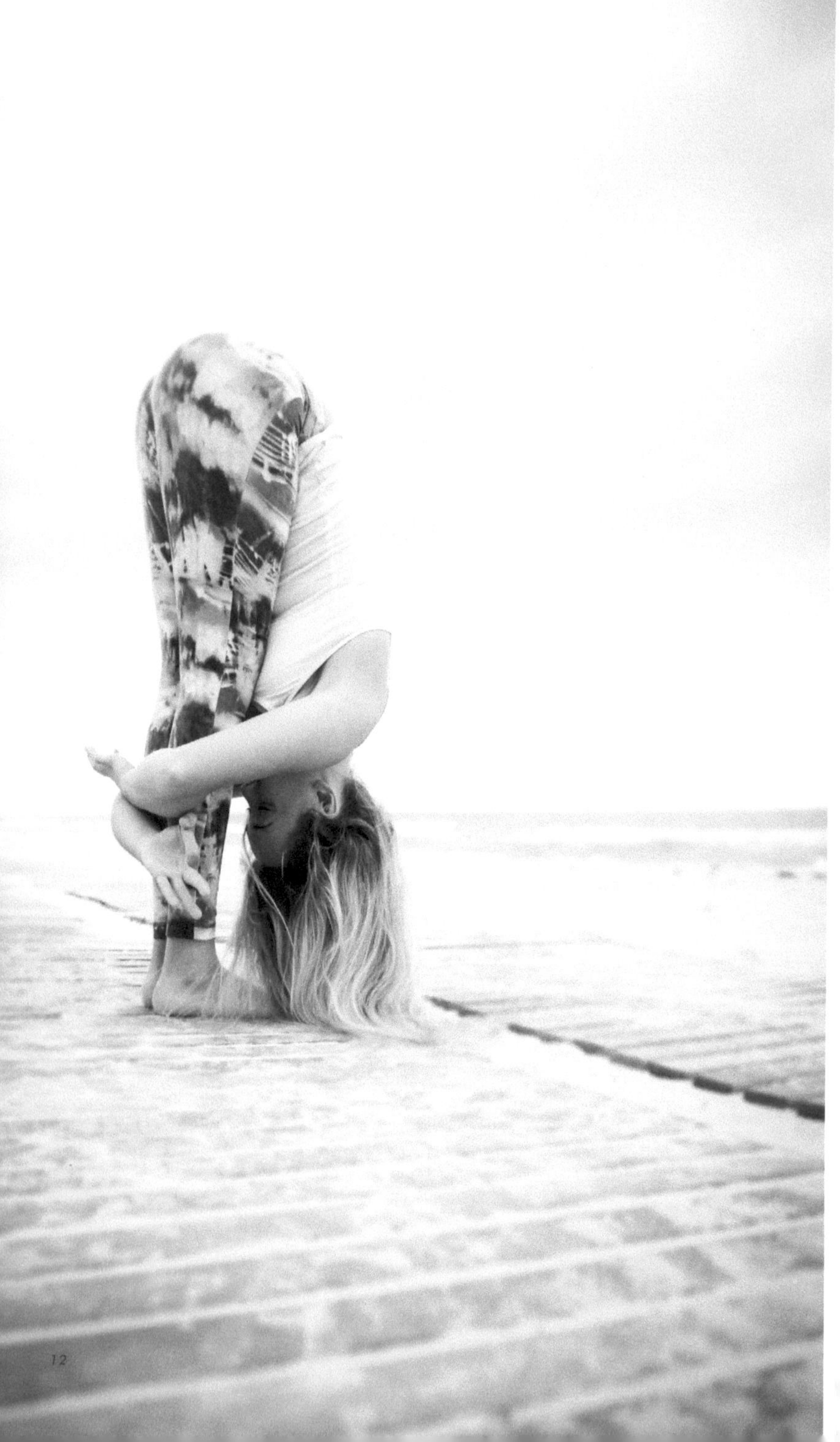

unearthed

unearth . . .   to uncover, bring to new light
here, as this monday begins its story
a visit long overdue
journey into me

here, in the company of these swirling flocks
in the sand
in the surf
in the wind and vigor
i meet myself

the veil lifting, guard coming down
here, in this clearing
the earth chimes in . . .
tells me to breathe, to flow, to sing, to allow, to celebrate
    and shine
this fantastic exchange of the elements not to be curbed

here, in these early hours
everything holy
unearthed am i
seeking no thing and finding me

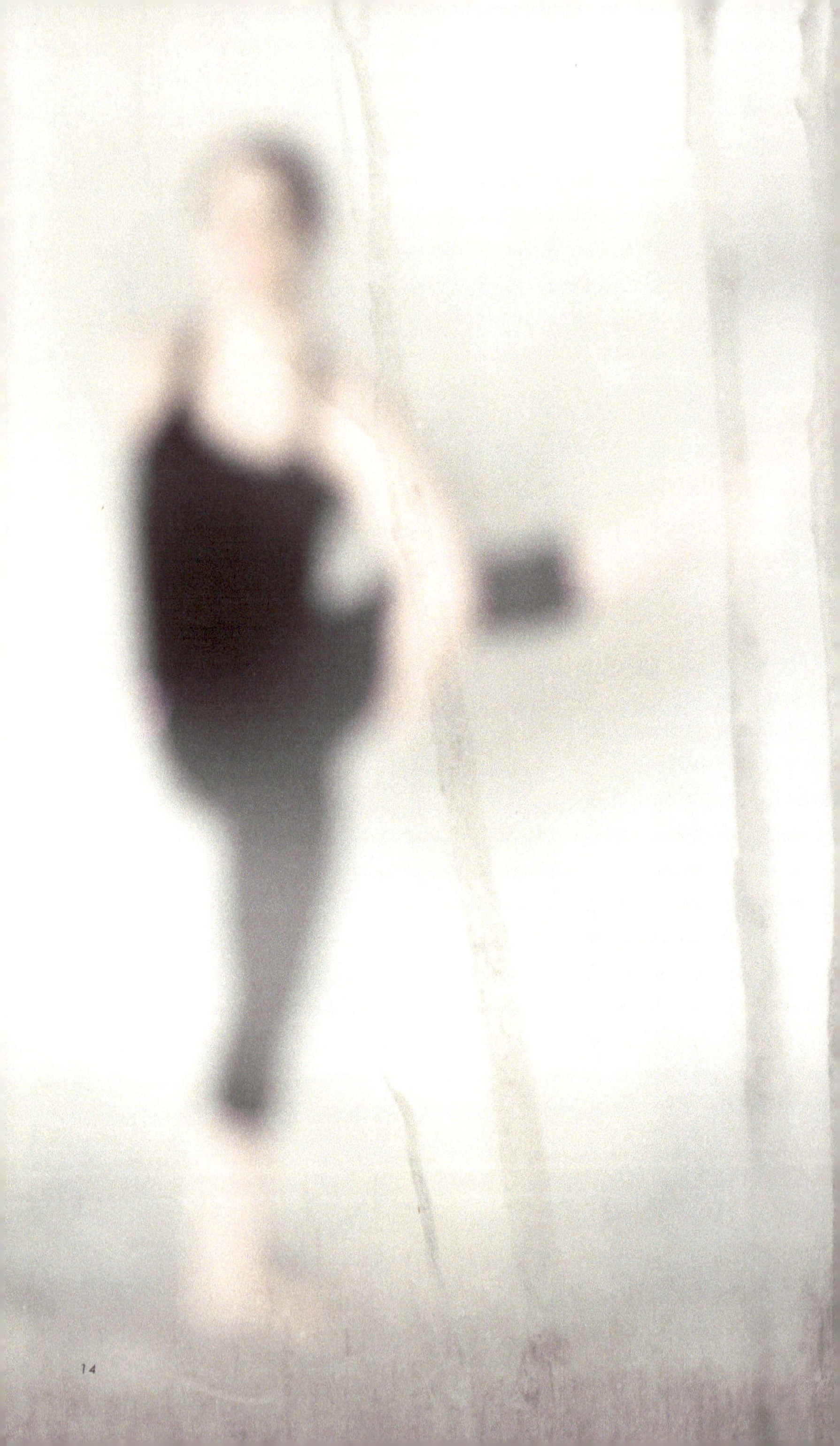

back to make believe

horizons . . .
out there, somewhere
today, i don't see any
don't feel their fence

here, up early with the sun
everything is possible
i am weightless and can soar
bring it all on

a spell has been cast
back to make believe
me with the cape and the magic

i come here to blink away the dust in these eyes
to take down some walls
i stumble and sway,
then once more find my feet
over and over and over

i come here to see out past
fields of NO and NEVER
to recall the beauty in trying

i come here to get going

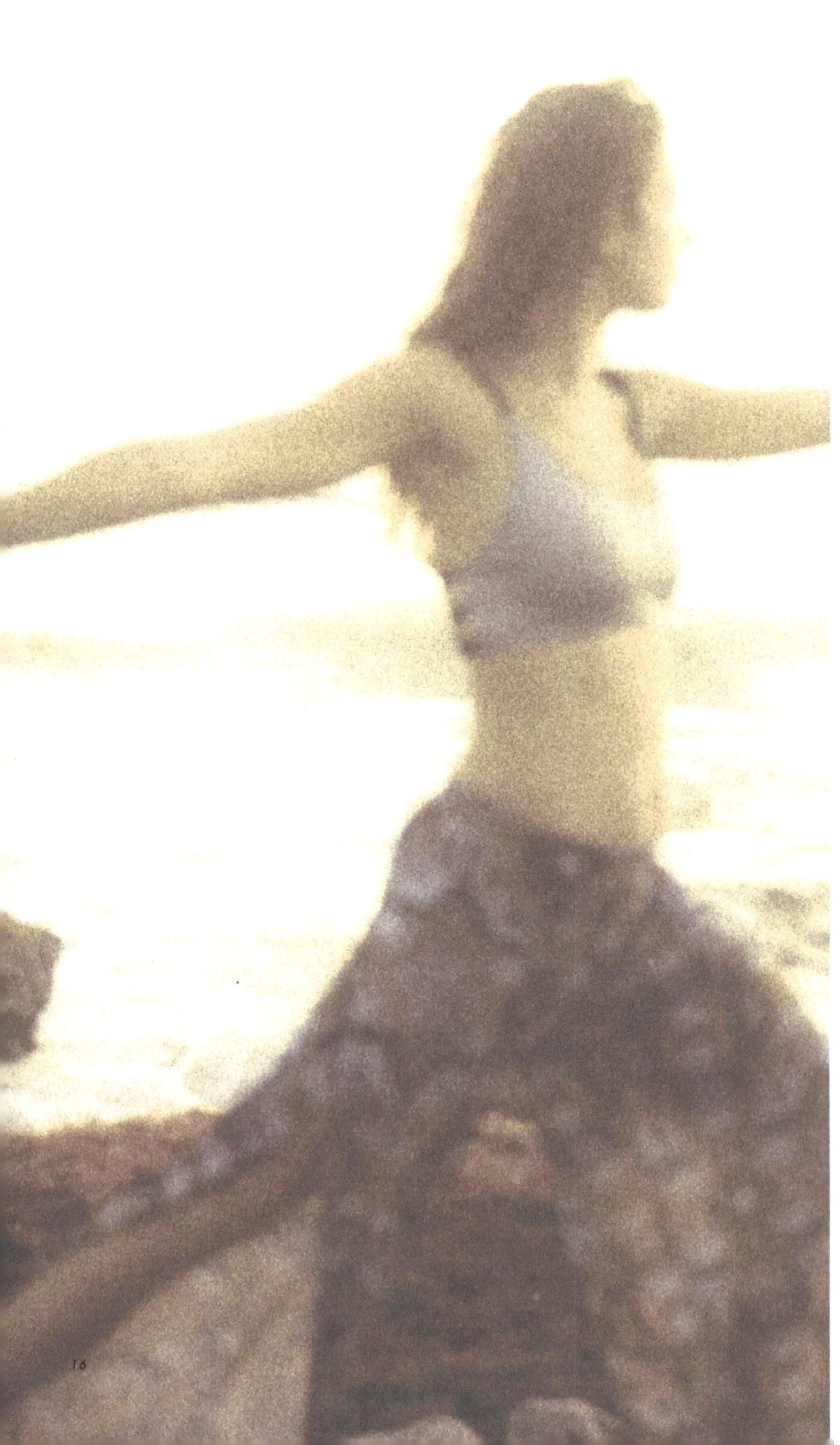

traction

affable . . .
i'm practicing being it
composure, and then some
in contention, not
a secret weapon for my belt

find me here, off hours
a party of one
repeating my scales
"teach us to care and not to care"

experiencing from the inside out
grinning at the thorny
faithful to the process
extending my horizons
widening the intervals between swerves

rehearsing for my tomorrows and the next
not to make flawless . . .   no umbrellas when it comes to life
just some advance planning
advance planning for the rush and the push
on demand, sands shifting, buttons pressed
then the skid . . .   into habits

a little stronger every day
and something interesting happening here
who is this visitor called traction?
composure, and then some
in contention, not

quenched

buenos diás
blessed . . .   so blessed

cloaked in the elements
beams pierce through vapor
the breeze rippling palms

salt water tumbles rocks
raging, then hushed
currents . . .
like my mind through plans and schemes

but no pouting from the sea
and, oh the sun's optimism
then there's the wind . . .   forever following through
day in, day out

and so my weariness begins its pivot
once a jungle, now an oasis
the fog burning off, composure sneaks up
quenched, here in this simple study of morning . . .
all I really need to know

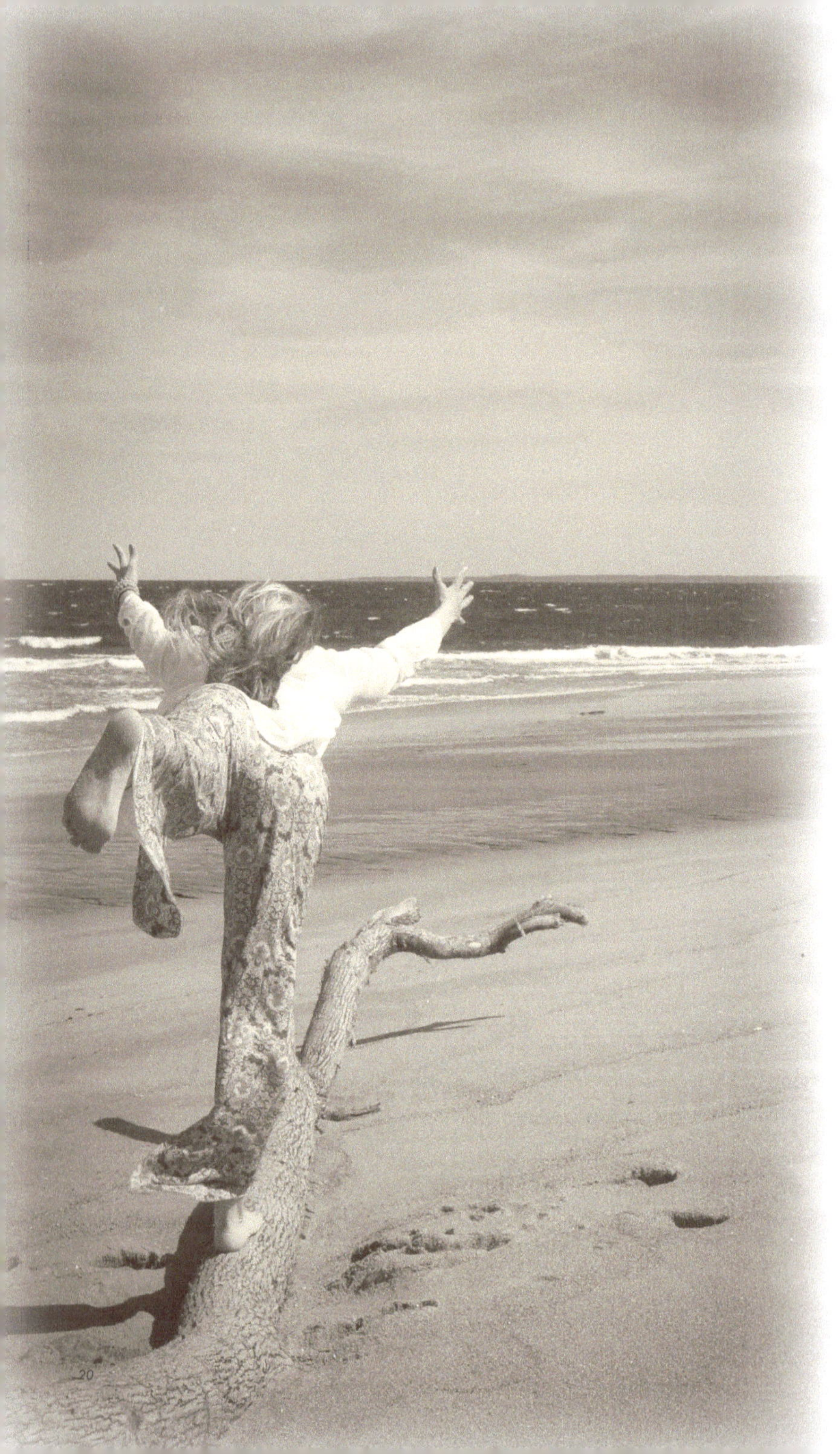

gamble

believe ME, they said
I heard, question . . .

they said talk
I heard, listen . . .

they said rush
I heard, linger . . .

they said fact
I heard, mystery . . .

they said first
I heard, last . . .

they said borders
I heard, roam . . .

they said shout,
I heard, whisper . . .

they said viral
I heard, anonymous . . .

they said ME
I heard, universe . . .

they said perfect
I heard, unfinished . . .

they asked why?
I asked, why not?

they said same
I said, ME . . .

they say safe
I hear, gamble . . .

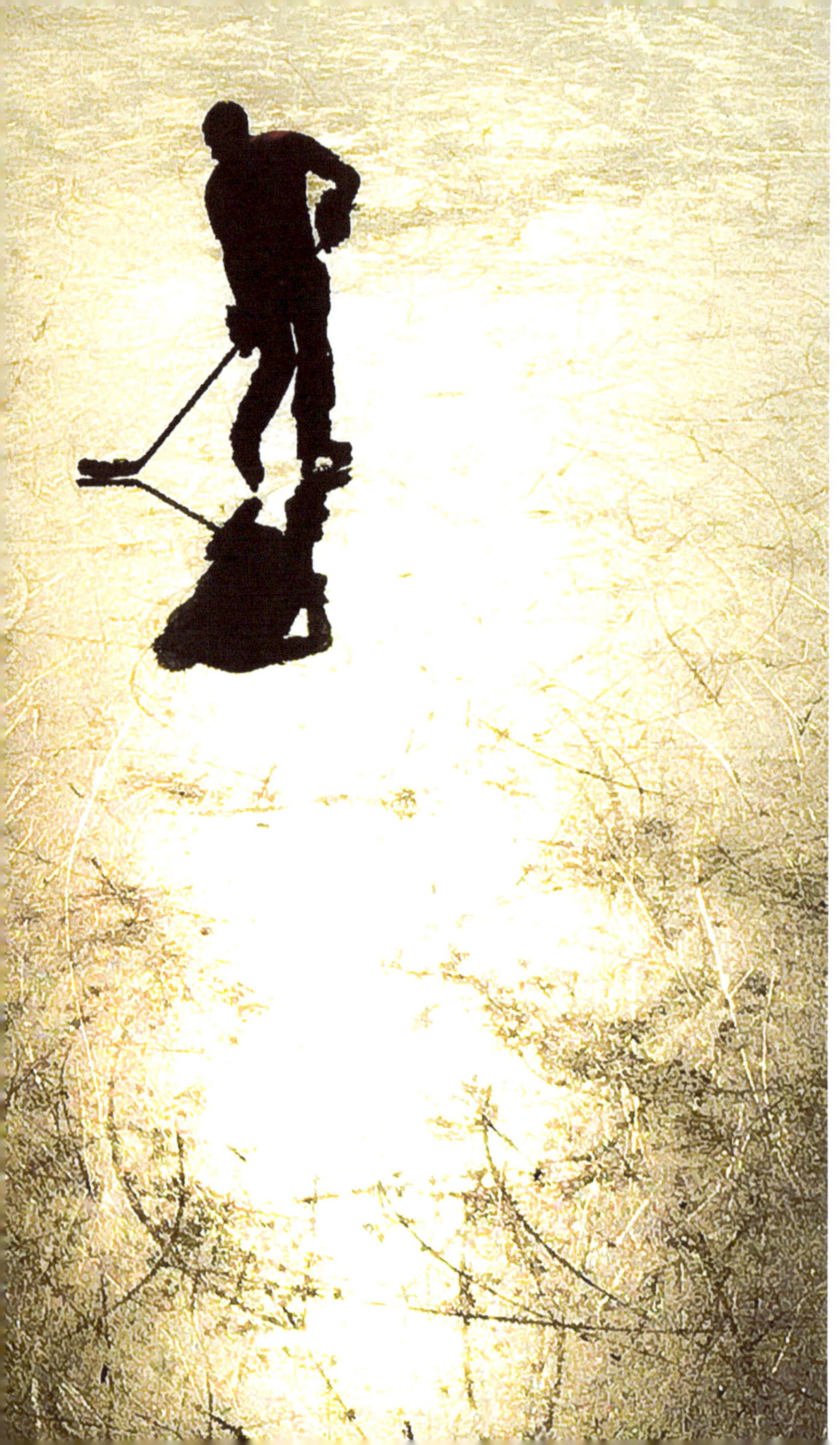

luxurious even

true this repeat visitor came barreling in uninvited . . .
forcing a pause and snatching eight precious hours of daylight
the bandit of february

but on this morning after, the sun calls again
as if to say, the coast is clear
a bright white canvas on which to chart the day
here to stay
not cold, not hot, just soft . . . luxurious even

in this shimmer of a new day we make peace with this
uninvited guest which has caused all the ruckus
stashing it in piles,
attempting to craft some order
we build things
we carve it

with a clearer lens we remove the temperature and see it in its purity
for really, what else is there to do . . .

the nomad

ah, but what of preferences and our devotion to them?
the added yens that fuel the checkmate

right, wrong
left, right
after the dust ups, mostly it's gray

shimmering light
thick shadows
could not one realize the other

yet on we grip
crippled for the sake of our way
breathing but not living
sated but not content
sheltered but not secure
together yet all alone

three cheers for the nomad who drifts from the margin's
safeguard
the rambler who thaws having lost the confirm
trading "I" for "possibility"
he mines in the gradient
he trips up the others . . .
and flares a ripple

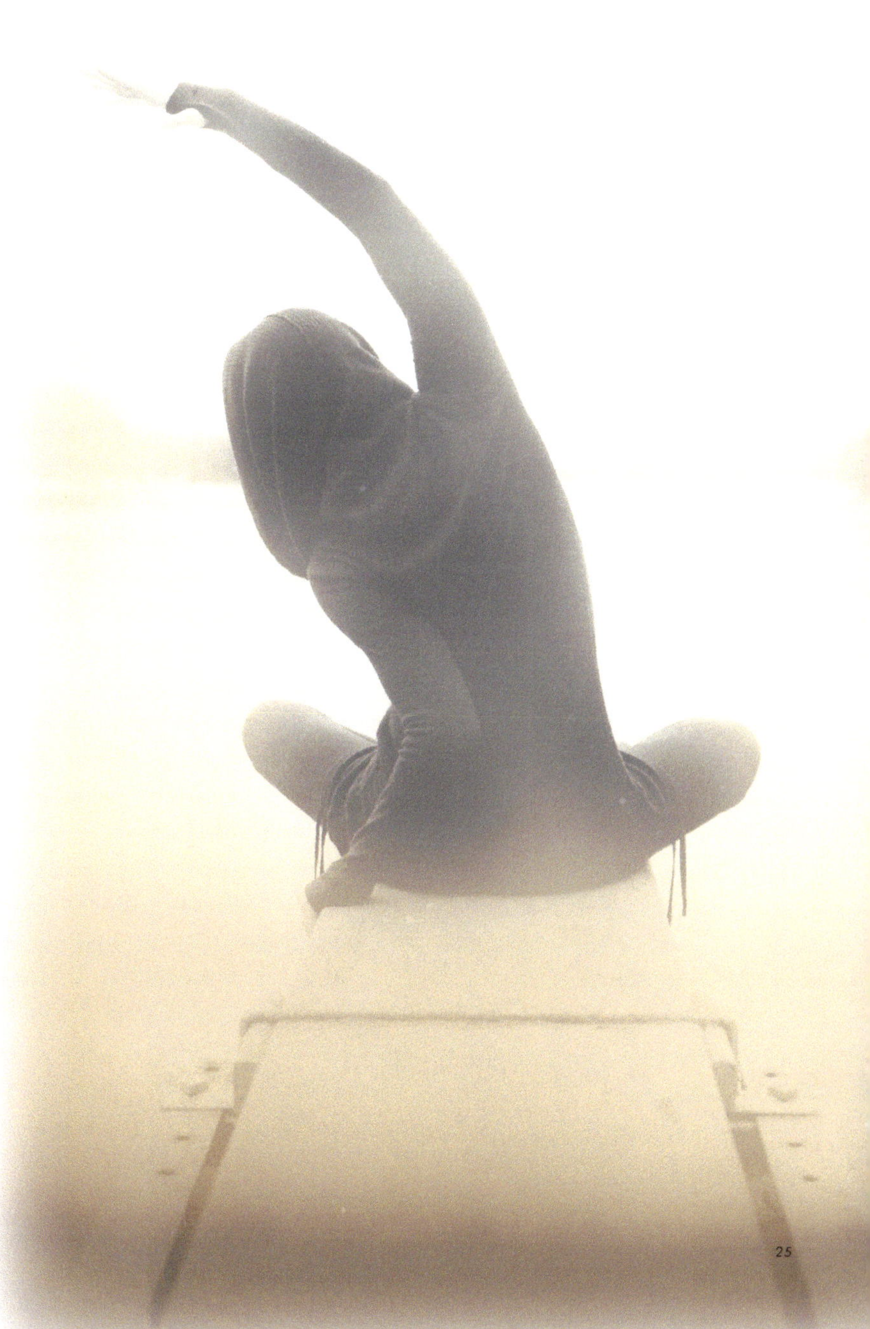

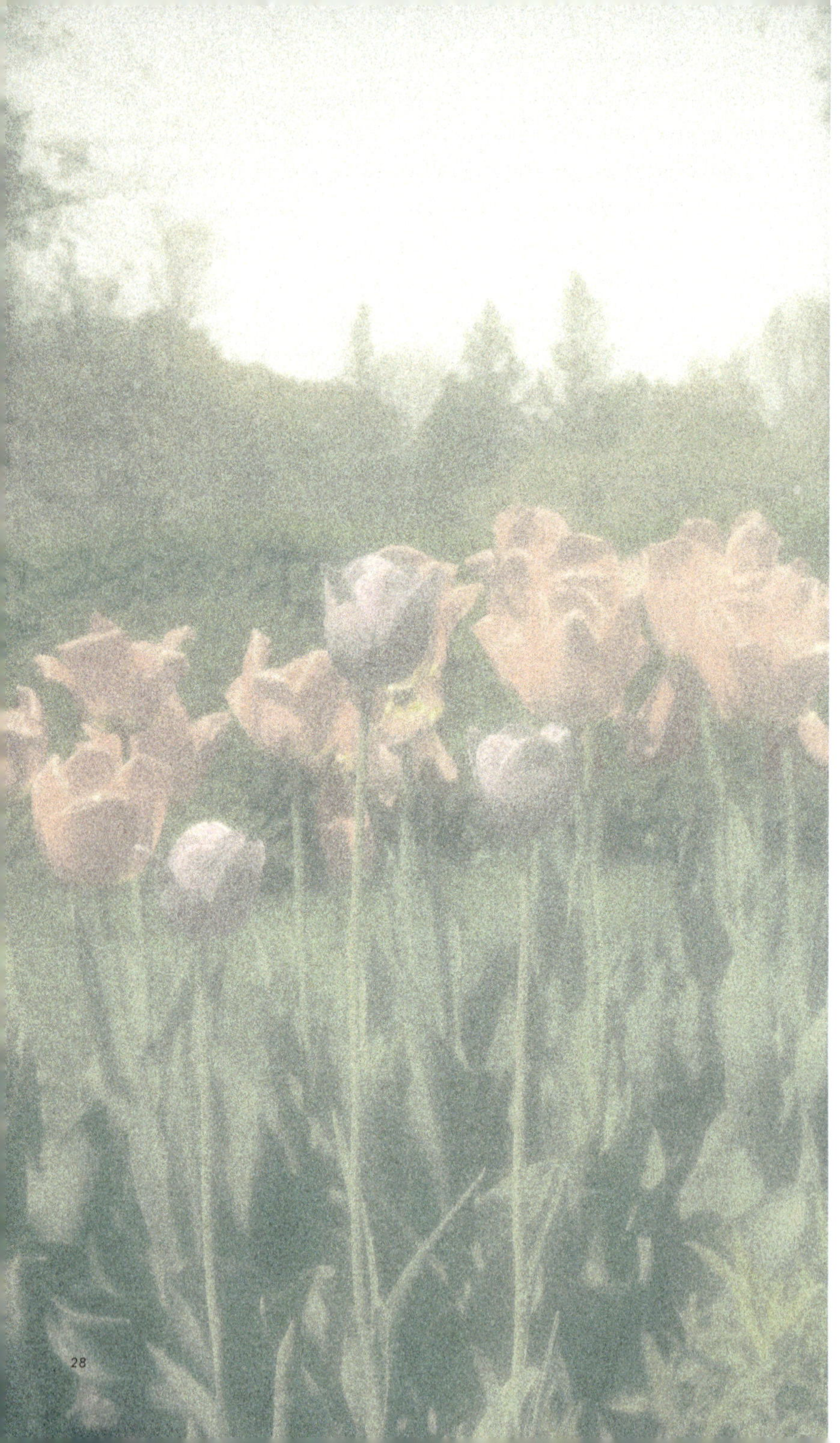

ultimately

yellow buses fetch
yellow buses deposit
sandals elbowed to the wardrobe's rear
streets resume their fashion,
and processions, once more laced with heed

september and its good mornings
big magic
the interlude where glory hangs in
fooled every year . . .
tricked into thinking the splendor will triumph

but shovels replace garden hoses,
ultimately
where bare hands and feet once communed
with earth,
there will again be buffers

great expectations migrate into mystery
layers off, layers (back) on
protests no match for peculiar ecologies
mere guests are we
yet every season blanks i draw

so up to the limbs and over the fields must go my attention
my teacher having arrived
blessings all,
"embrace the roots as the berries of june!"

farewell, for now
the cycles spin, revelations sway
but color follows the monochrome,
ultimately
kites will again flutter in blue skies
as will promise
layers (back) off, layers on

the thing with feathers

i heard it i heard it
the "thing with feathers"
long buried, its ambience
december, january, february and so

but just now, today
that "thing with feathers"
feet planted here in the truth
for certain i heard it
impossible and splendid and perfectly off pitch

and with my eyes
drip, drip, drip from the shingles
each splash chipping away at the stone

apparent too as i pierce the land with these poles
a journey from A to B into my grip
the "tune without words"
olé in this patch of earth long frozen

from vapor to beam to shifting sand
"in the chilliest land"
the passage
i taste it . . .

nothing quiets spring
this i knew
so why today so arrested in these tracks?
here among these trees perfumed by sunshine and song,
softly go the lyrics not to be heard through my yawning indoors

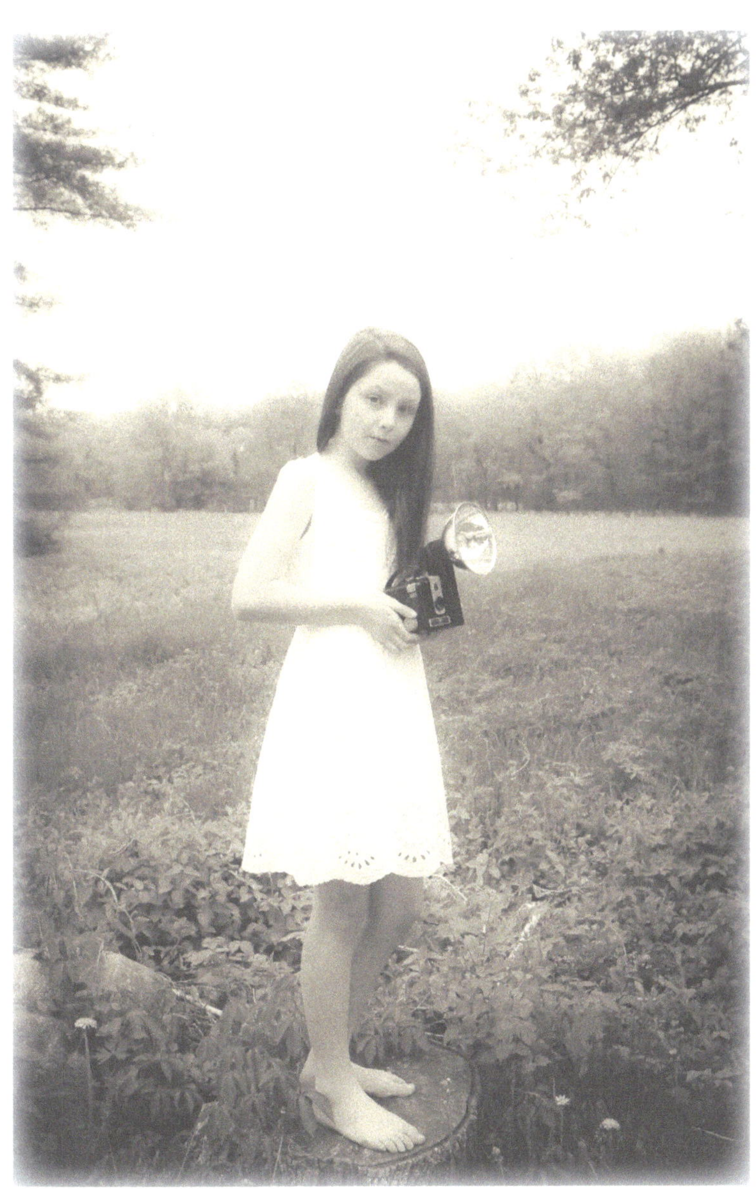

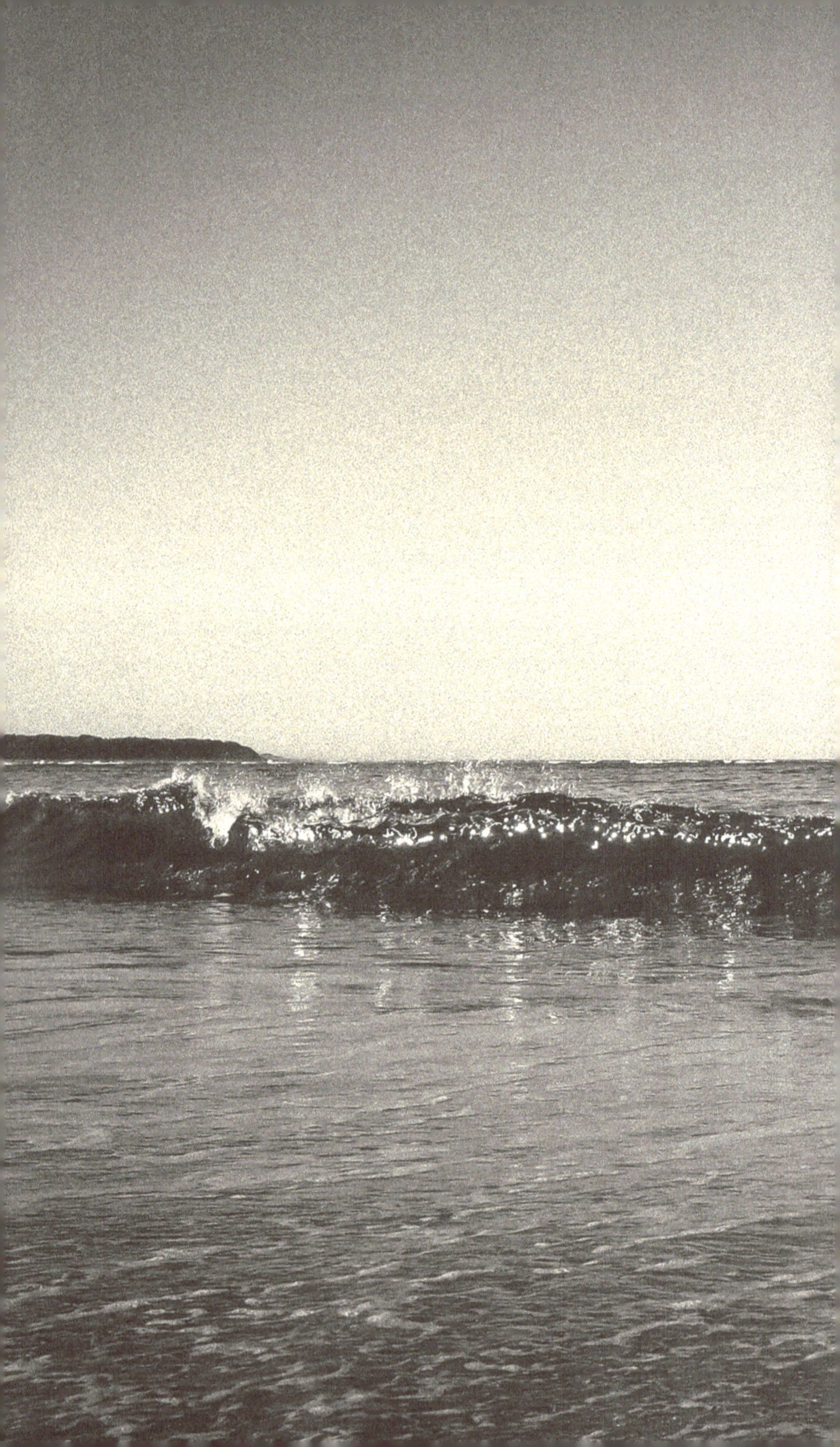

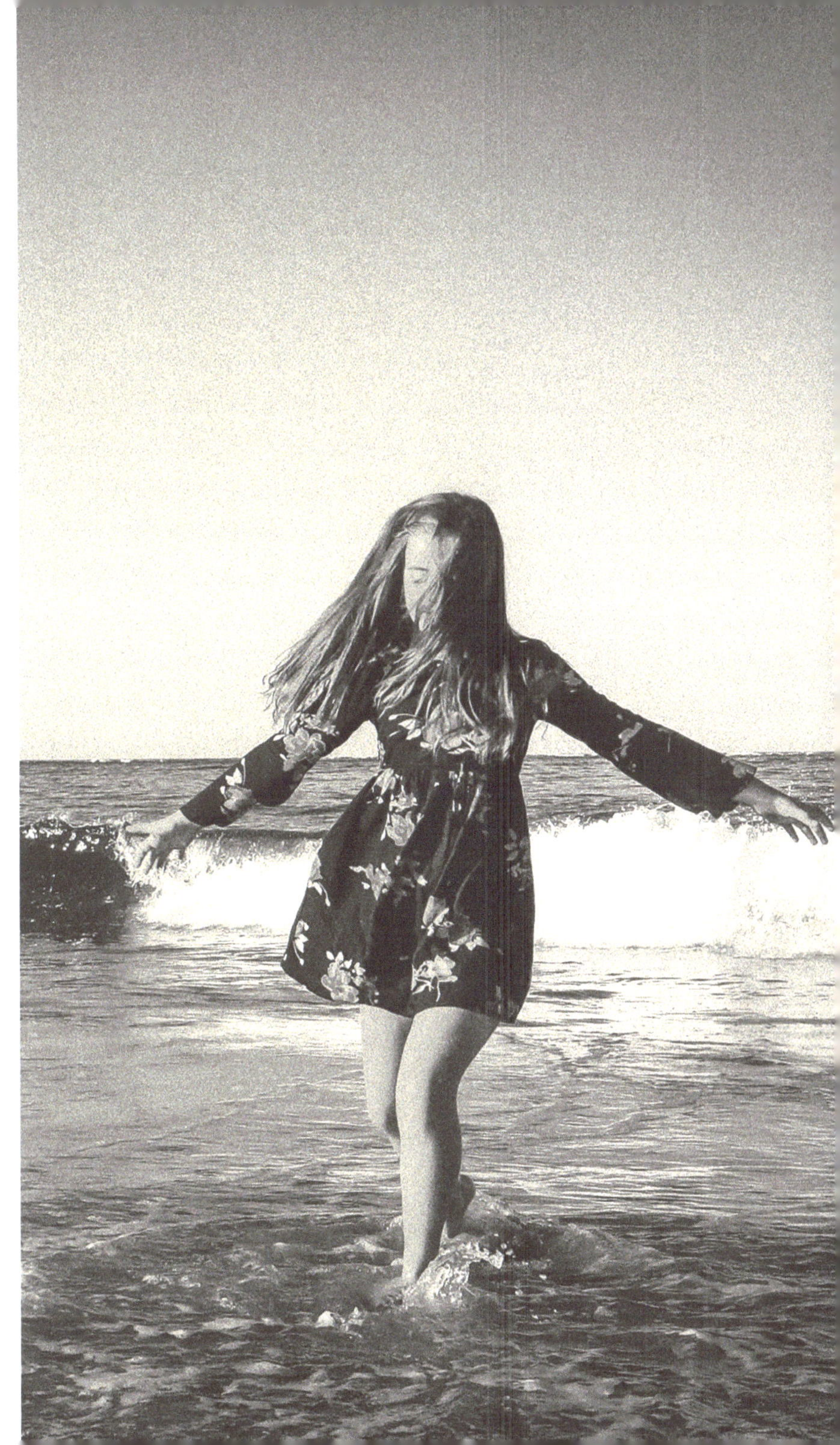

ten thousand, maybe more

this witness to being
heartbreak
fear
loneliness
forgotten

big circumstances
malignant
not willing to work it out
on the spectrum
position eliminated
stage four
he took his own . . .
totaled
not this time
not covered by our . . .
no survivors
in the custody of state

this happens
what doesn't kill you makes you
but what?
what of the space before the muscles take shape?
lives on the margins
hanging on for (dear) life

not to elevate
not to probe
the whys do not matter
just listen

the gift of silence
a blank canvas to coat

i see you
this matters
tell me
tell me your story

subtraction

it's what you leave out
removing those things that distort . . .
assumption & splash, ego & winning
the price we pay for amplifying

doing the math with each unfolding moment, distilling down
down to the essence
then, just as it is
enough said

being without . . .   without accoutrements and such in the sum
        of light
awakening to just this, just this, just this

how the glow finds me here in the reduction
the call and response
white so considerate, so candid
tracing somebody that i used to know

and in simplicity and all its pomp
in this sum of light . . .
equation solved

it's what you leave out, what is left unsaid
this is how we arrive
this is the sound of less

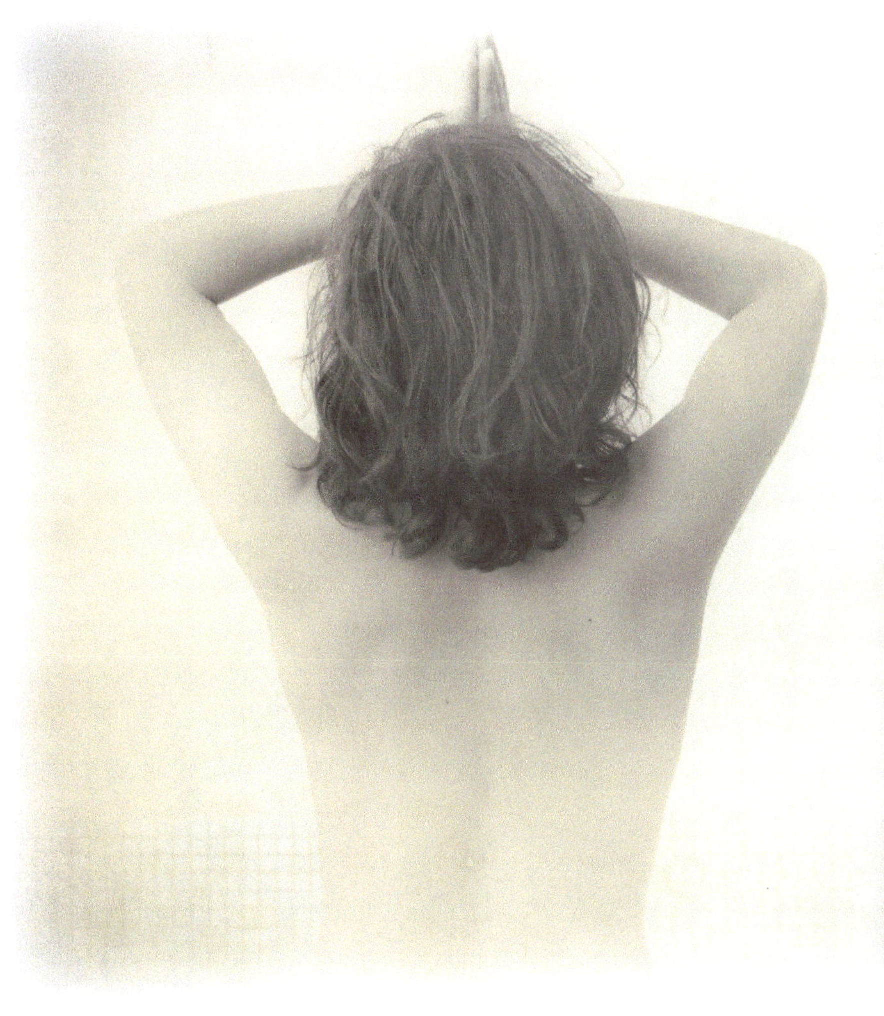

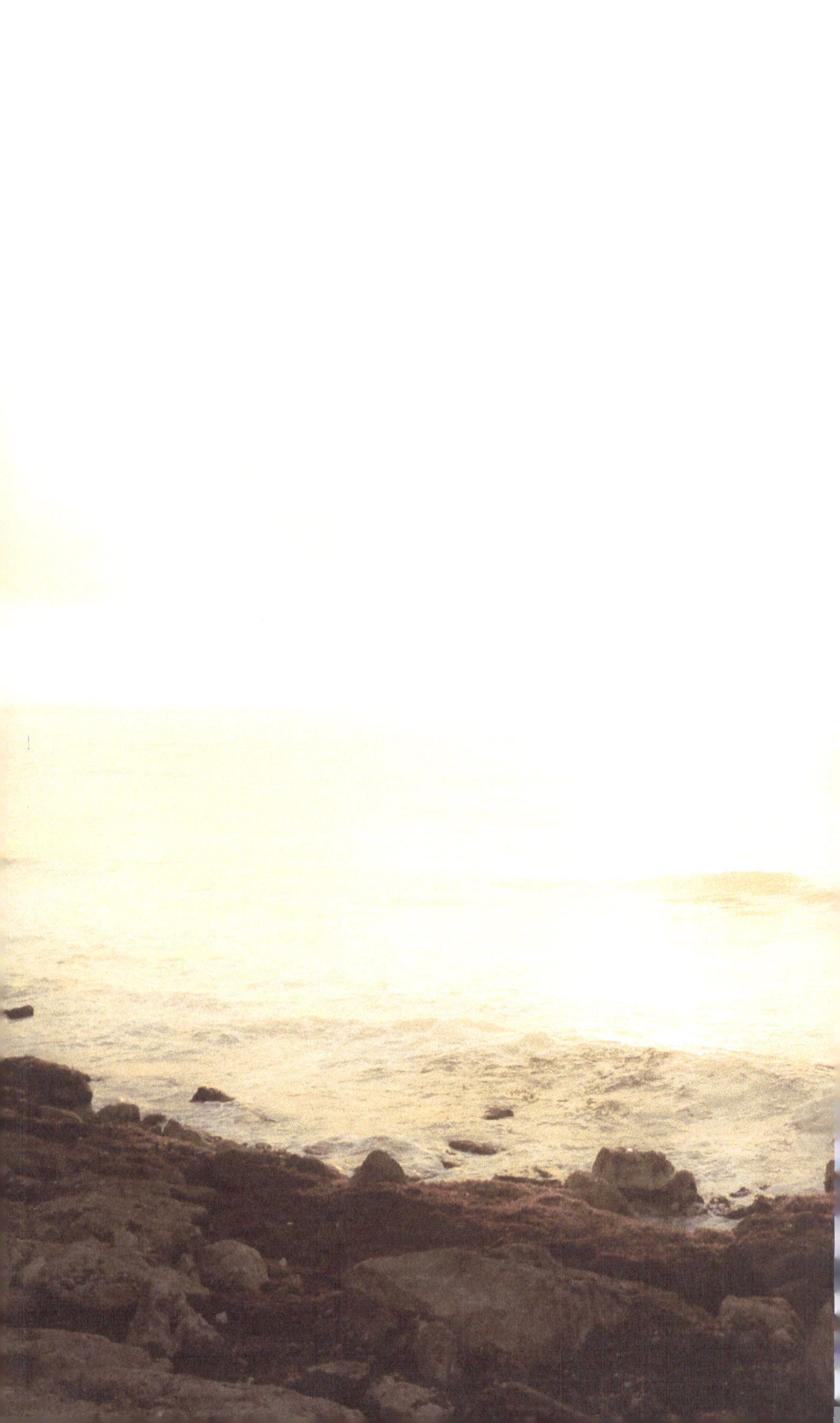

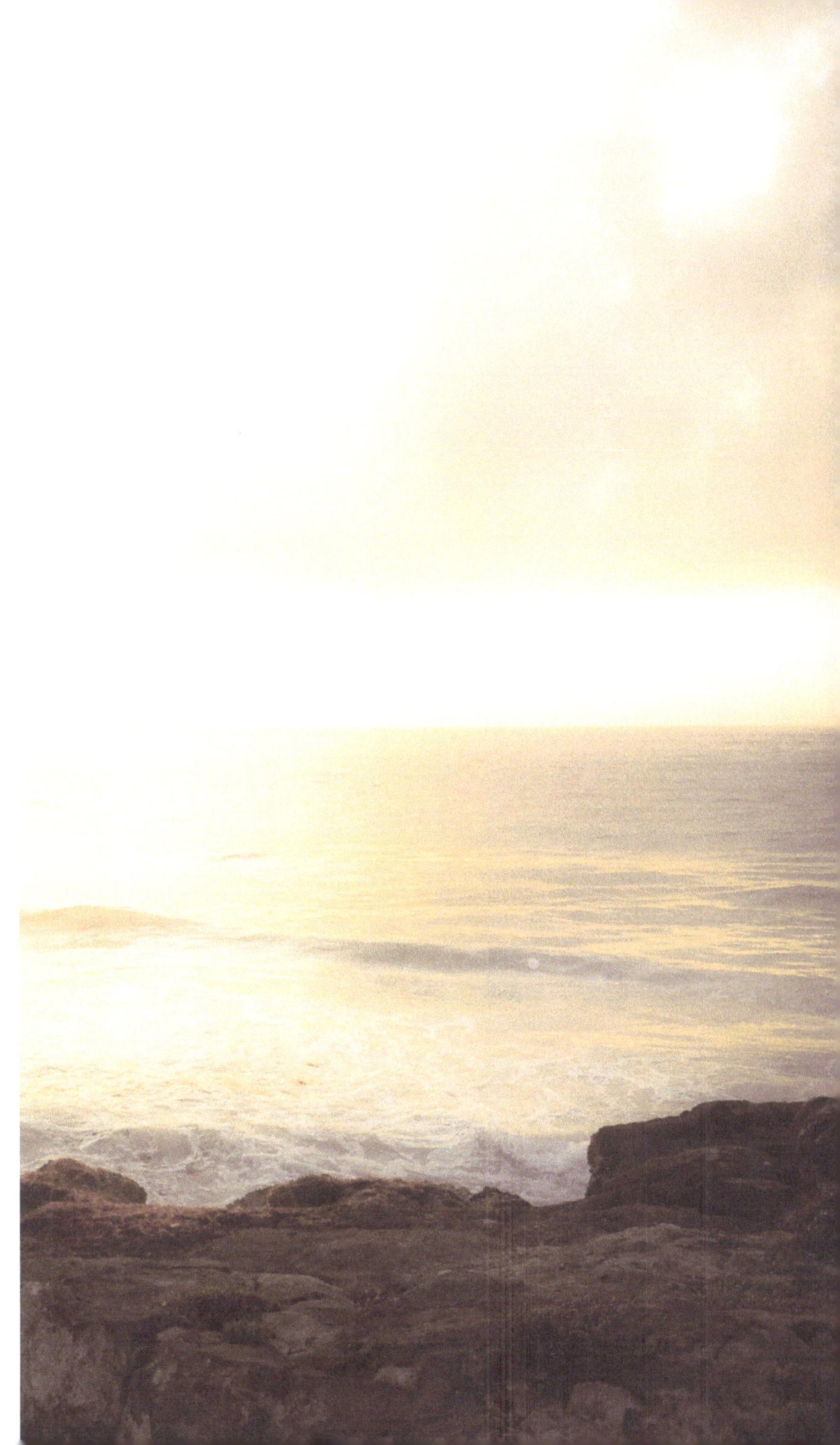

the lilacs, for instance

windblown, midnight jasmine, ocean star, amber moon
        . . . vessels brimming wax
plunging our faces into interpretations
summer honeysuckle, coral harbor, wild sea grass, ginger dusk
the string ignites and the fantasy swirls in widening circles

but it being may, ditch the understudies
follow me up the bend to central
up where we can reach them spilling over the pickets at the turn
where we can gather them up in our palms, imbibe them
as if for the first time
astonishing ourselves at the source in just a few sniffs
uncompromised . . .
glory, glory, glory

among the traffic, the clutter, the chaos of it all
miniature propellers clustered softly as a team, here and there
the grape or ivory bringing radiance to the greens
the only expense our heed

come and amble just for a bit, claim this
their vigor fading as the days extend
in springtime at 3:30 in the PM . . .   why, why hesitate
especially today with their tomorrows few

make perfect the effort here
or, out the screen door to your own backyard
they all chant the same mystery
for tell me one thing
one thing that might trump this?
enchanted but for a moment, here in a classroom called present

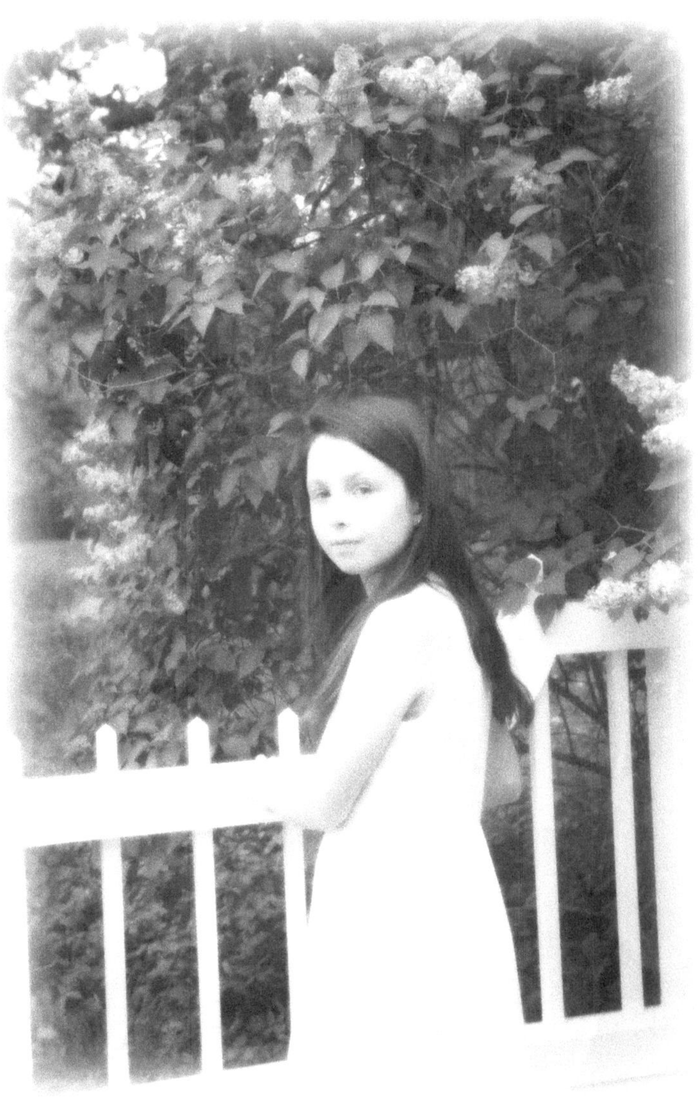

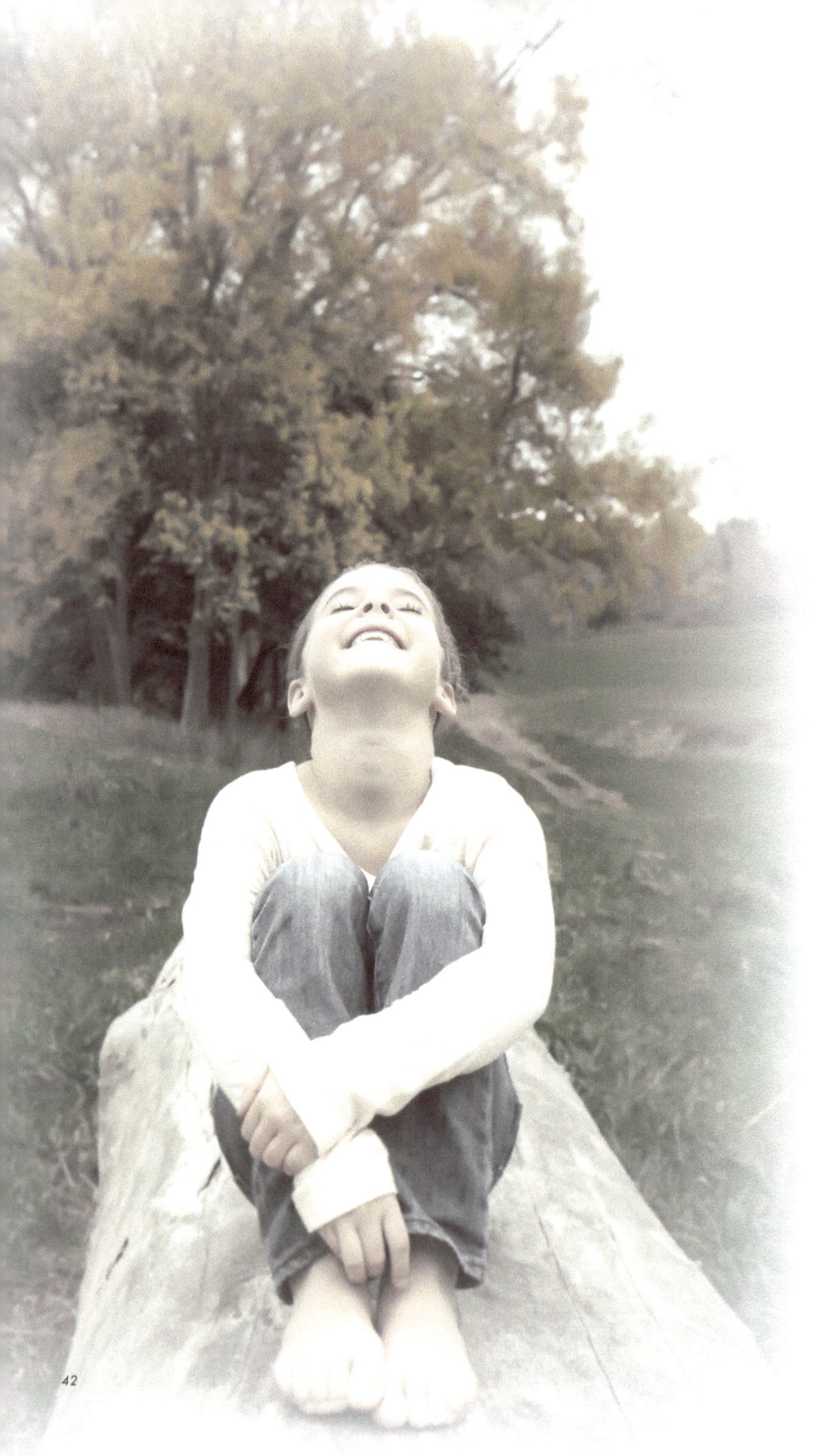

second nature

how these summer blades of varying heights and widths so
masterfully, so effortlessly
. . . catch the beams from above
second nature
close to perfect as is,
yet just now fresh from their drink, nudged into majesty with
the sun's dressing

same goes for this water gushing at my right side,
and the day lilies at the turn
a bit more fancy for the dawn
but this morning
today, i'm charmed by green
by the seasonal
the ordinary
patches, tufts dressing the chipping curb
and, not missing the simple gift of light

gets me wondering
could i meet that promise?
that elementary promise of doing no more or no less than
catching luminosity
that same light just now warming my shoulders
allow it to affix to me
draw out some good for the others?

despite conditions
despite disregard
despite being stepped upon and spilled upon . . .
in seasons high, seasons low
amongst trespassers
can i muster the might to just present myself to each new day
not miss, not postpone the gift of light
repel it back in some way that only i can

surely that could be a start?

robes or no robes

call it prayer
call it metta
call it grace
call it . . .   manners

you don't need a pew
don't need a cushion
don't need beads or a preacher

"thank" and "you"
all the difference two words can make
not to mention "hello"

all comes down to paying attention
all comes down to compassion
this basic consideration . . .   of others
switch the me to we before the word matter

every face deserving of a read
every voice an ear
every set of eyes a lock
every life a witness
the finish line is for all

share the merit
say your rosary
behave
give thanks
do unto others
salute the sun
chant
drop to your knees

at ease
at ease
at ease
for the benefit of all

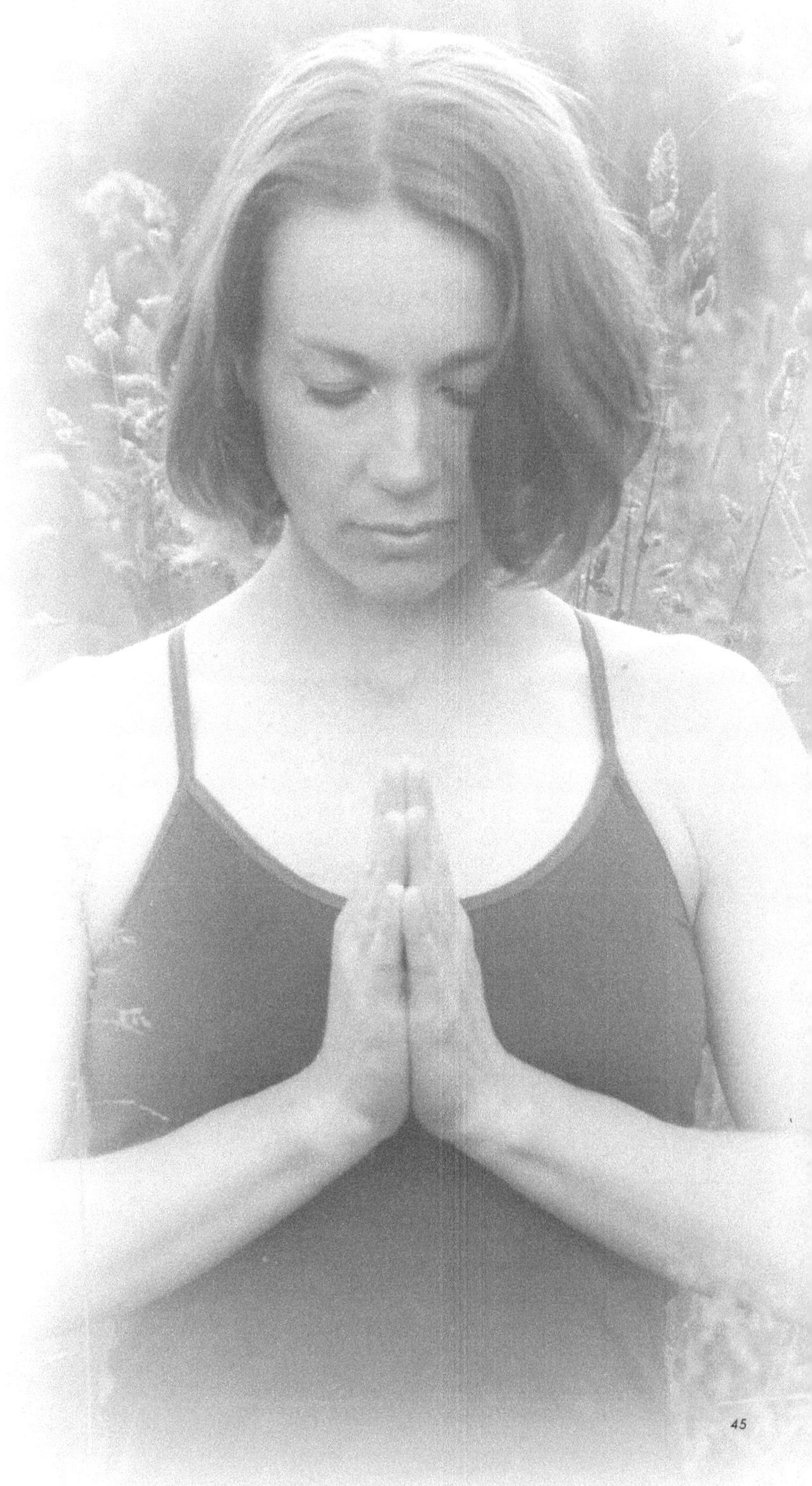

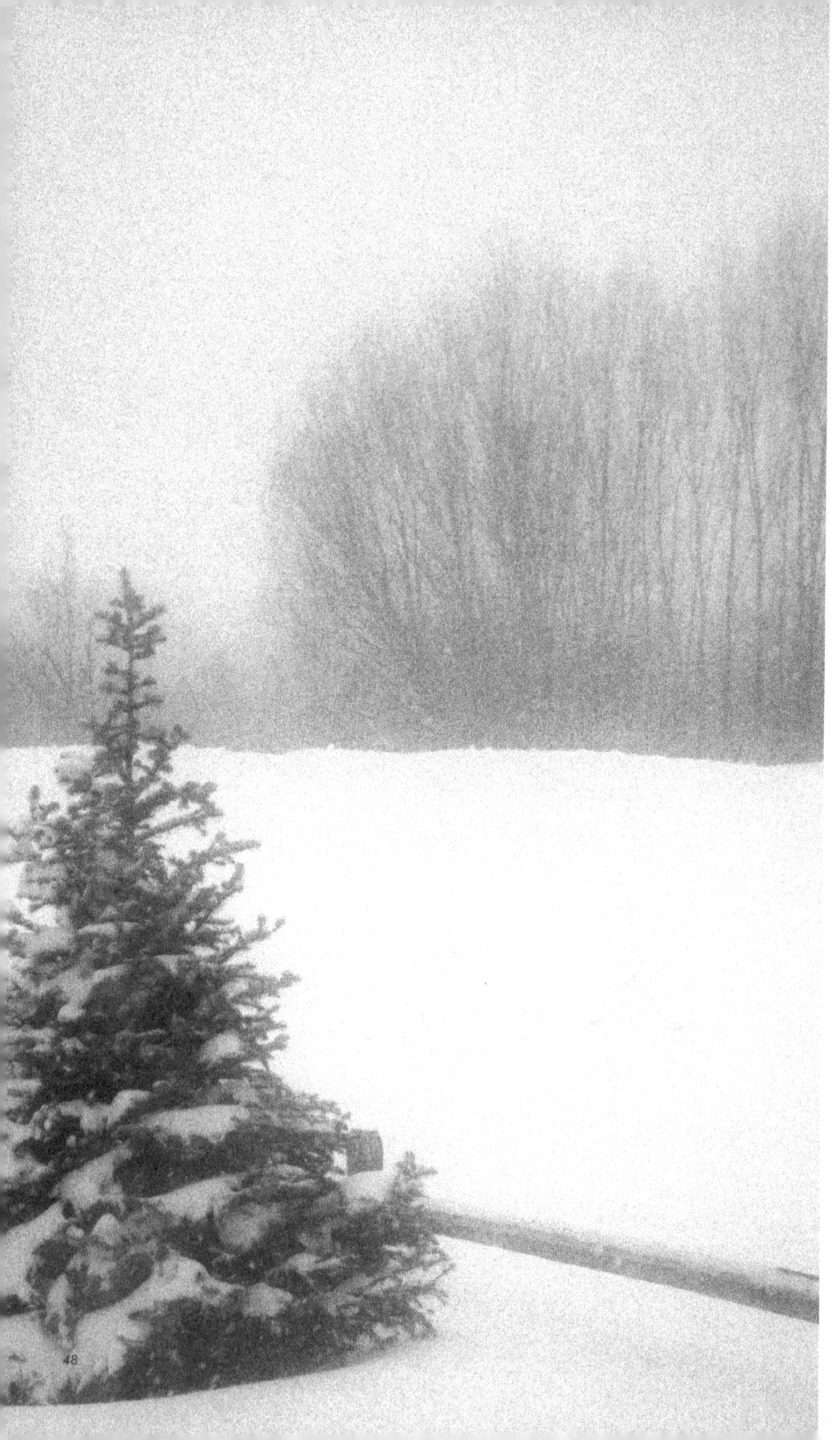

phased not

another light commands
and me, late for my lesson once more
hold it
right there
not so fast
winter's linger
take that
and, then that

the sprint halted
plucked from the tended village of the certain
my opponent this charmer with the edge, no match
grumbling at the hands

white, not green
frozen, not fluid
bursts and gusts and detours
gray not blue
grains of white tumble from the bleak
again today, tomorrow too

then out the window near the desk
i catch glimpse of the tree
two eyes close, then comes sight with the other
we lock gazes
my dissent silenced

nothing ahead, nothing behind
phased not
just here
beauty in the alliance

roots of rhythm

breaking day
on the edge of some universe . . .   this mist of salt, sea, vapor

a veil of quiet tucked below the call and response
gulls and otters command the soundtrack

one, two, three, four . . .
sages of wings and beaks and whiskers squawk in quarter time
stealing a patch of this earth as my classroom . . .
ME the trespasser
the property all their's

breathing in . . .   exhale rambling
over and over, my anchor
arriving
the earth rising up to meet me
senses filling
state already altered

one breath, one motion . . .
what was static becoming now fluid
this canvas of stone basks in the rising shimmer

breath in . . .   glorious
exhale stretched
me in the neighboring surf, the surf in me
its cadence inclines me to an alternate view

through crown and hand i snatch the mighty from these
elements
feet in the clouds
head in the earth
coral beams meet sodium air and contain this field of presence
this field that for this moment is me

pose sculpting around breath
the sea suggests a lightness of being
inhale, softening . . .   exhale life coursing through my limbs
diving deeper
planting the seeds for my thursday

ever brightening, my song raves on . . .
heart greets sky, saluting majesty
this clean slate my tattoo for the hours yet to unfold

downshift . . .   back to the start
the effort falls away quietly as the background in some photograph
my lesson now finished
roots of rhythm escorting me into my day

one, two, three, four . . .
they of wings and beaks and whiskers carry on with purpose, as will i

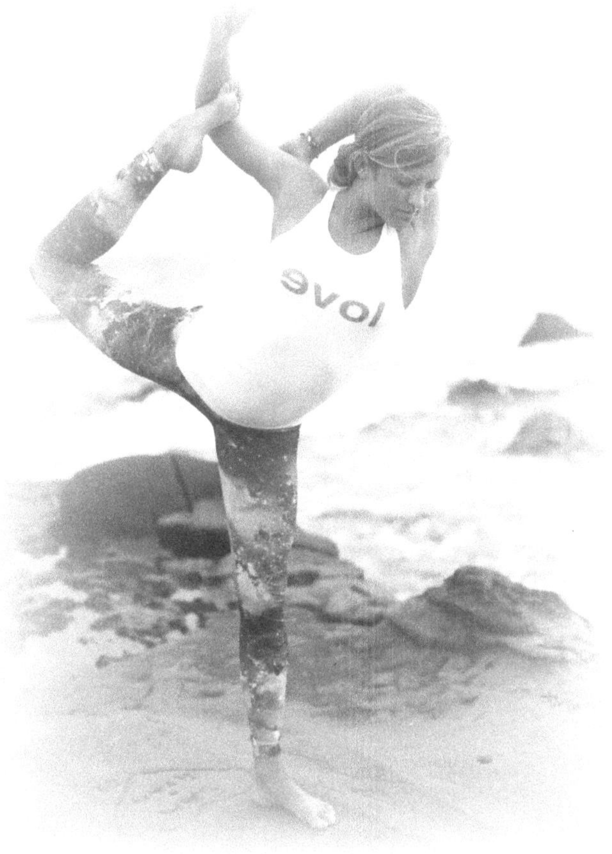

optics

confront my lens
never thought of it this way
like some battle to be fought

a match?
you and this piece of glass
let us go a few rounds
then, with the armor off
a few more

only a contest if you say so
but to me
i see it
this mirror perched between us

to me it's but a hammer for these walls,
this fencing for safekeeping
something better to hear you
a doorway through which you may pass
or, i

sway into a clearing where we meet for the first time
after the extra rounds
and in that (comm)union
a document
revealing who can say what
just some thing lured

some body tempted
tempted by the quiet chance of being known

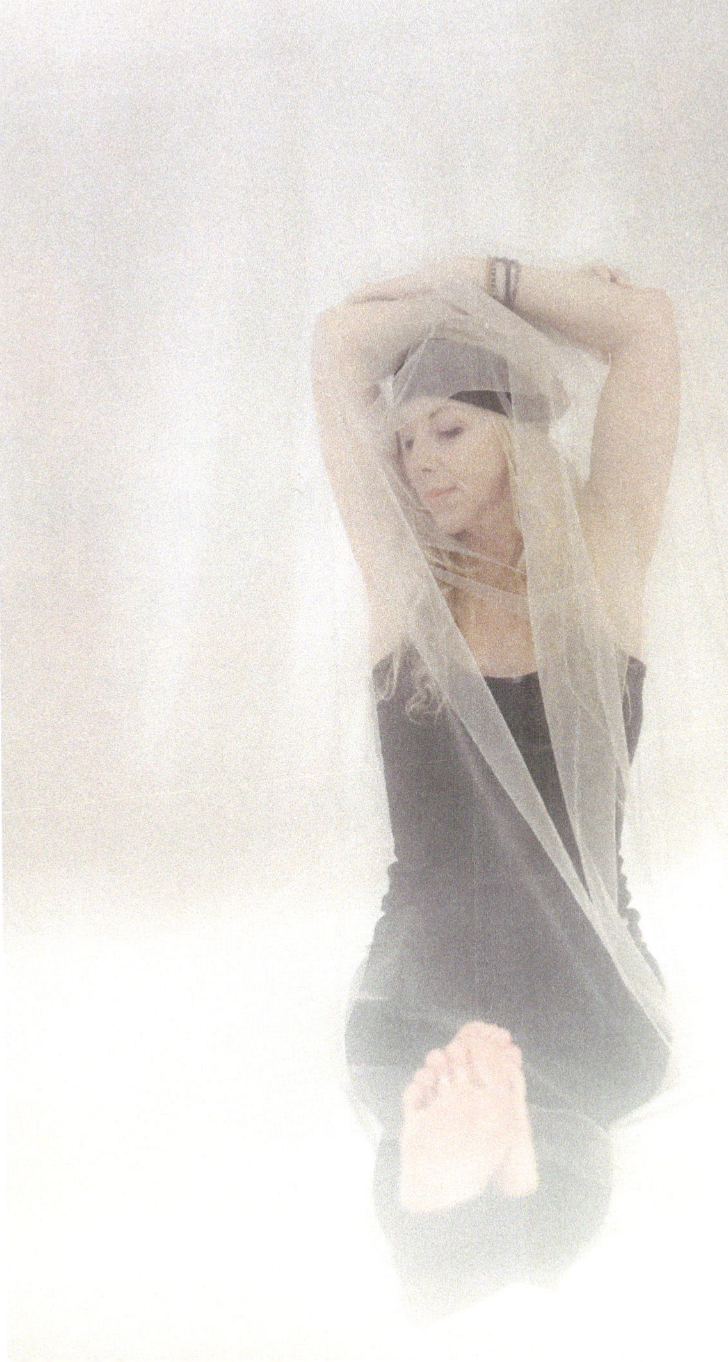

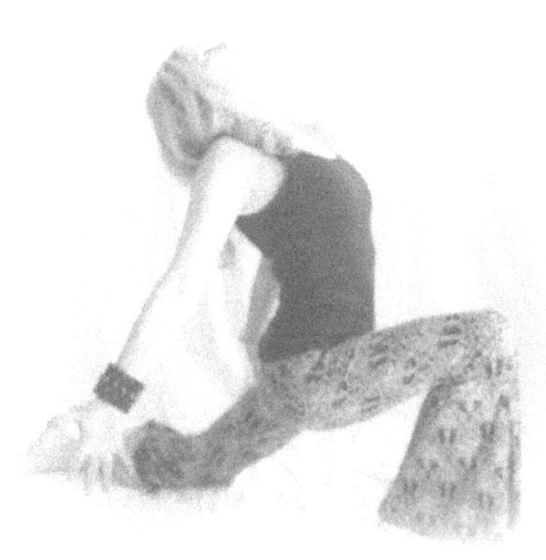

only human

the ten things i am never without:

1. my children
2. morning
3. preferences
4. a picture
5. sound tracks
6. a heart, breaking
7. inquiry
8. a calling
9. thirst
10. the looming arrival of otherwise

scenery

land-scape n. 1. a section or portion of scenery that may be seen from a single viewpoint. 2. a picture representing such scenery.

purple mountains
grand canyons
"diamond desserts, wheat fields waving, dust clouds rolling"
scenery . . .

contours of earth and sky. but, my lens for many years directed elsewhere. blind to the word's figurative definition, "i don't shoot landscapes . . . ", my standard. "it's portraits that i make." yet the more i sit with these glimpses of spirit, i question the accuracy of my stand. for in these faces, these figures in practice . . . am i not documenting vistas of another realm? so too divinity beams through these expanses.

your land
shifting sands
peaks and valleys
at work, at ease
scenery . . .

like a tourist arrested by the view, compelled to stay am i. to record this terrain of a soul. trees and mountains. the rugged, the polished. figures posing majestic in the light, and others there quietly in shadow. what of these parties of one exposed through my lens? what to label the pictures that represent *this* scenery. these images surely some testament to a pitch?

perhaps, i stand corrected . . .

blur

the edges blur and sometimes more
softly goes the focus
journey to the heart of the frame

the brush fluid, even clumsy
wandering the canvas
minor characters taper
all eyes to the essence

melodies collide, the compass abandoned
deliberately meandering the bends
not bothered
seamless instruments singing
bewitched, bewildered

adrift in the posture, unclenched
roots extend, earth rising
limbs sprout, floating
a heart grows edgeless
a kind of heaven in the gray

armor down, recipes vacated, expectations shrugged
yielding yielding yielding . . .   to the process
the uncommon order of things

a clearing where the light creeps in
ferried to some higher ground
the soul splashes
this is how the potions brew

changes everything

there you are!
in through the back door, fashionably late
almost didn't hear you

you, with your boundless heart
dropping petals
perfuming the breeze
and causing all the ruckus up in the limbs

your worthy opponent, so loyal to his teachings, finally takes
    his leave
out like a lamb he did not go
after months and months of hammering, winter's tough love
now the days ramble a bit
changes everything
again, things seem possible

so, tarry not
he'll be back before you know it
come in, come in
you and all your charms
teach me again . . .
remind me of the other side of sacred

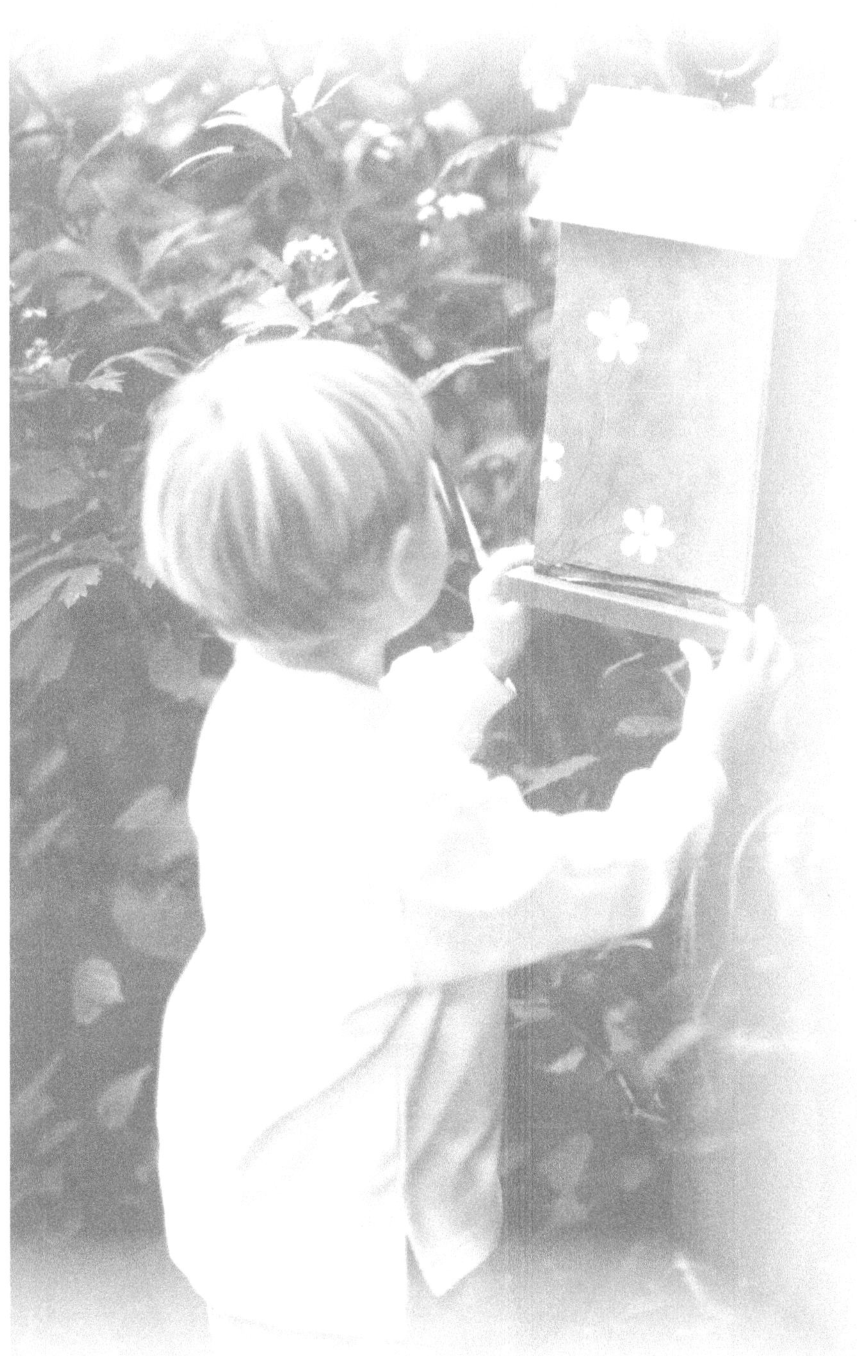

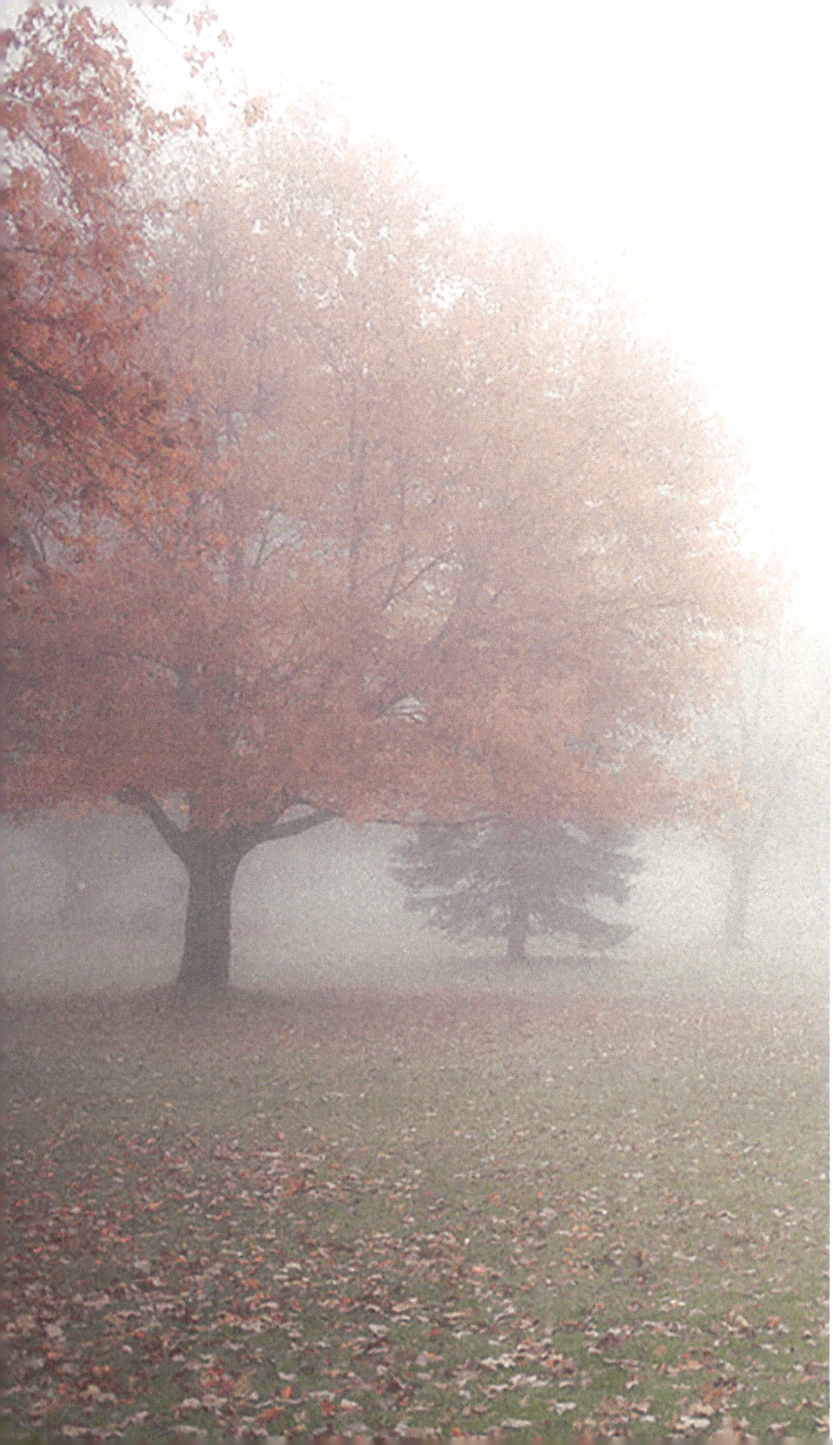

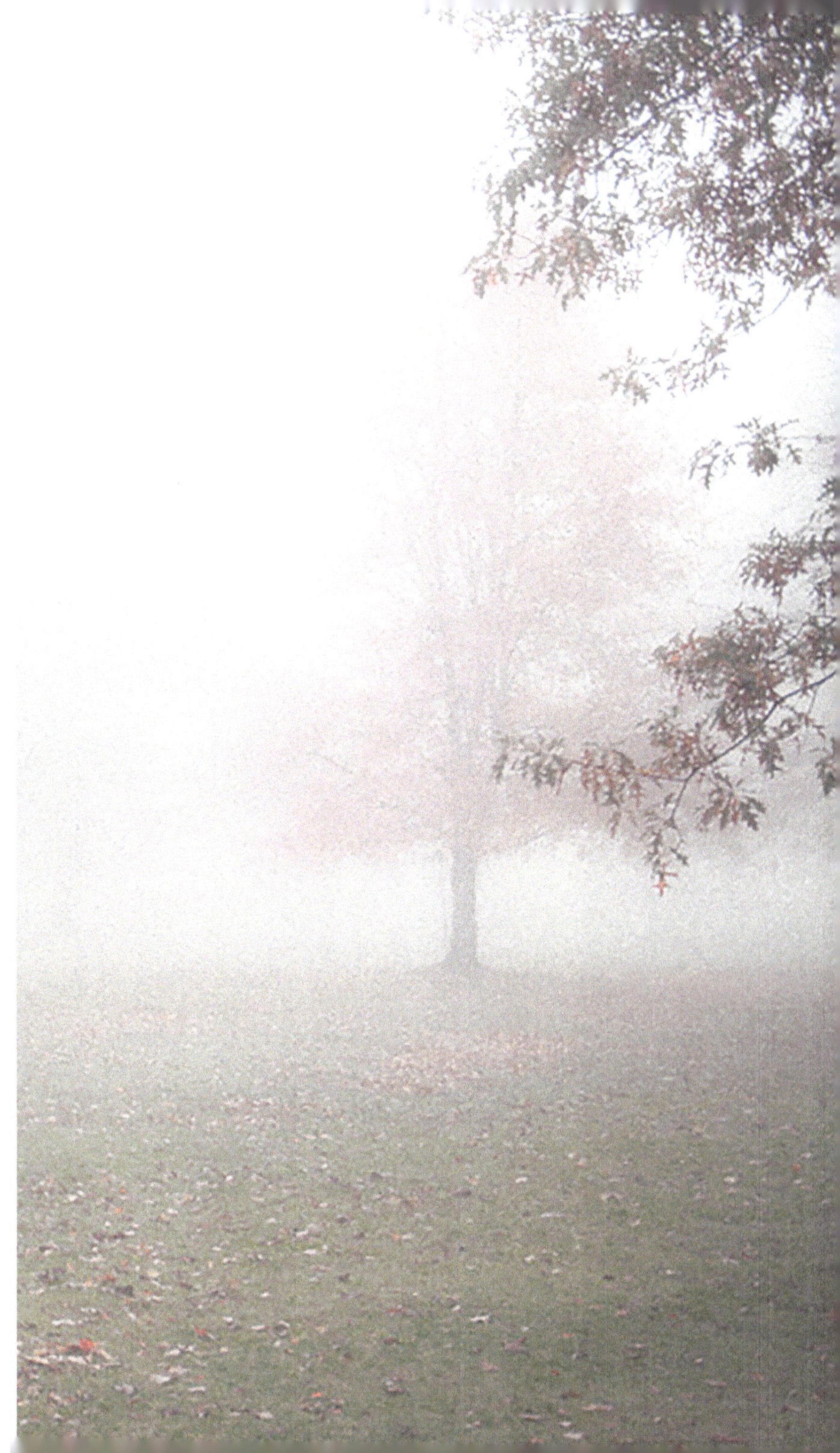

re *pose*

i could stand here as i do, mostly
attention adrift
vacant
"this body running sore in human form"
accidental me

or,
the other option . . .
i could yield to place, simply
survey *my* land with absolute attention
arrive and address this ally called now

seated or supine
i could take up foundations,
map the triggers of that study
a detective with his clues, forging connections
a-ha

up *right* rather than down *cast* i could be, mostly
but that would involve a split with frenzy, departures, mirage
customs i blindly go favoring
up *right* . . .
that would involve remembering what i knew

i *could* yield to place . . . simply
in motion or fixed
i *could* take up foundations
forge connections
re *pose*
a-ha
"whom should i resent when pain occurs?"

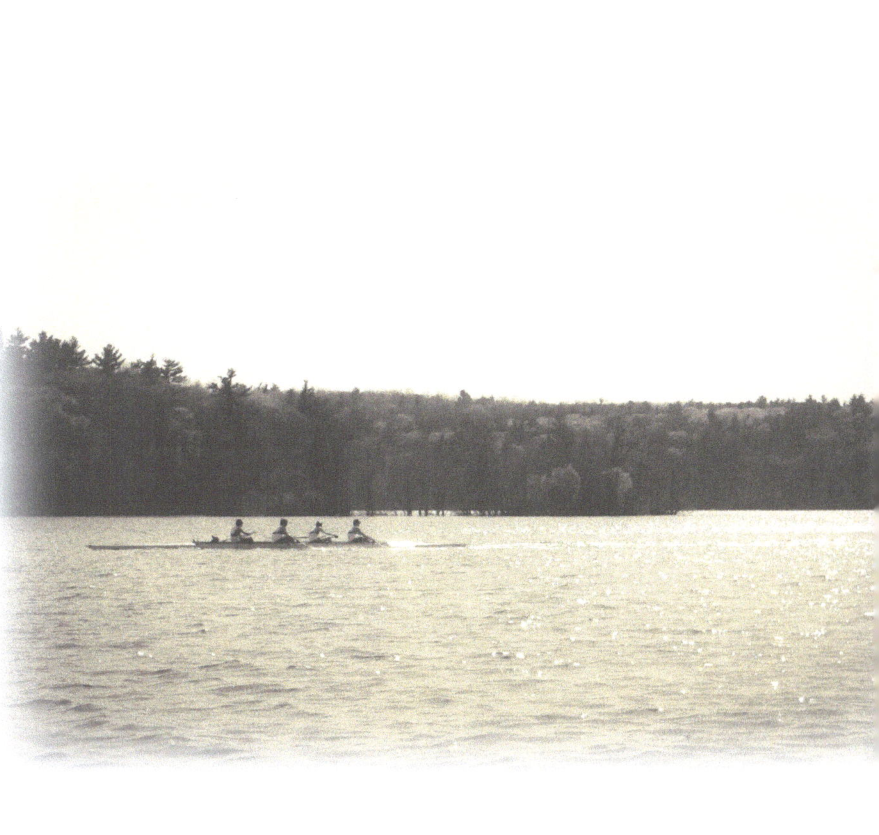

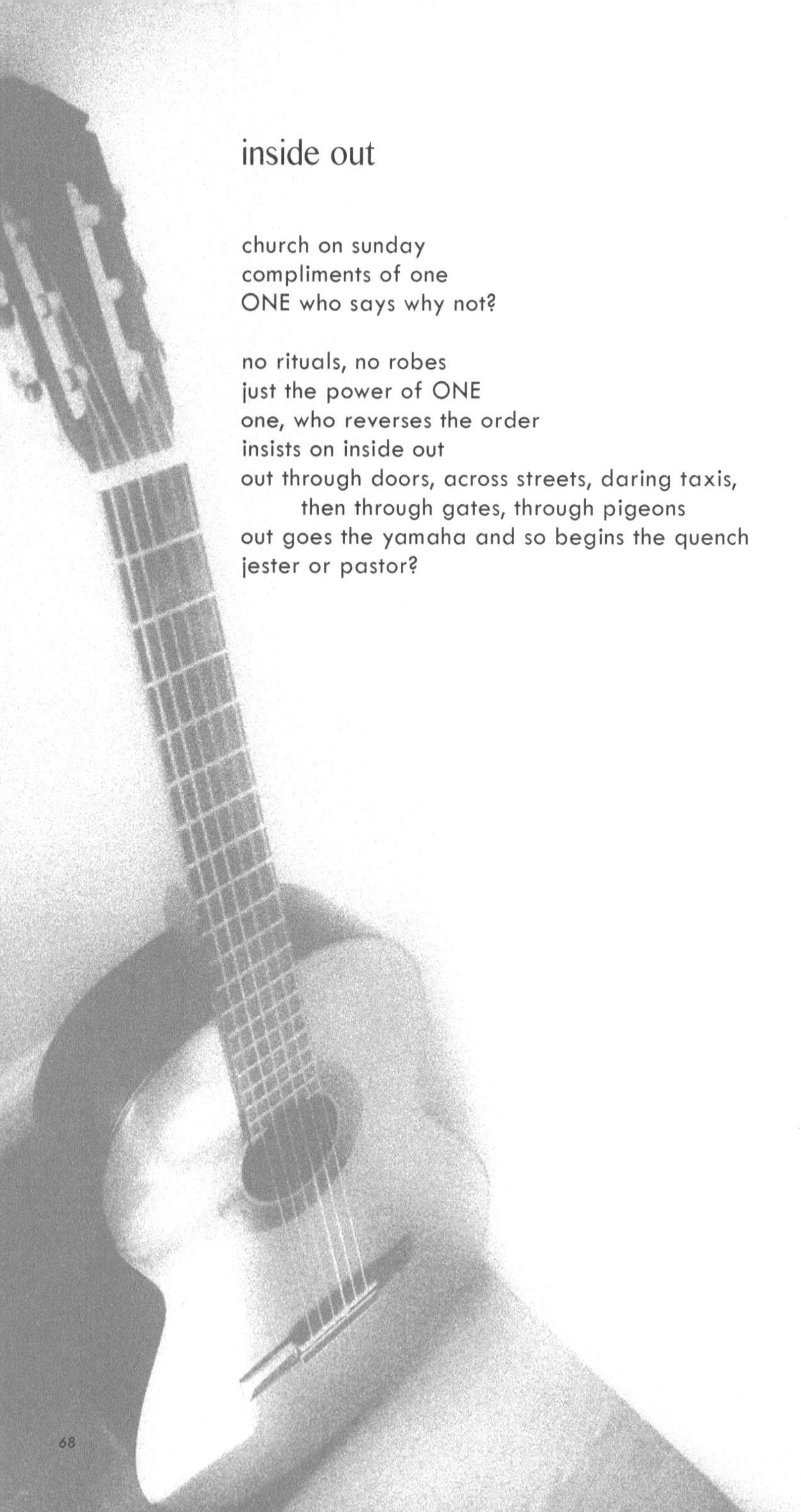

inside out

church on sunday
compliments of one
ONE who says why not?

no rituals, no robes
just the power of ONE
one, who reverses the order
insists on inside out
out through doors, across streets, daring taxis,
    then through gates, through pigeons
out goes the yamaha and so begins the quench
jester or pastor?

with this, my peace i grant you
edgeless in the minor
haunting and blessing
blessing and haunting
up the scales, then the descent
bits of chopin, glass, "hallelujah", satie
cathedral ceilings shed their gospel above

in mystery and speed we gather
harnessed
lugging bundles and babies and books and chums
lugging mistakes and blame, messages and reruns
depleted bewildered beguiled
lured by the keys' sure release, the impossible beauty
of song
peace is possible
better than right, better than first, better than mine
bless us in our trespasses

pivoted back by simple gesture
the burst by ONE
back to a humanity shared
for an instant, stretched
and so a ripple begins

be seated,
but for a few bars, completely unburdened
be still in your sway,
witness the maestro's softly weighted hands carve
be here,
with eyes and ears and every cell,
imbibe this covenant
give yourself
follow the thread to offering

sweet spot

here with these lids heavy . . .   can you see what i see?
which is not;
fences
plans
wrinkled hands
doubt
myths
fear
NO
tomorrow

see it, can you?
horizons endless
freedom
enough
belief
truth
audacity
YES
now

my hands in the earth, the earth in me . . .   can you hear what i hear?
which is not;
adrift
better
if only
should
why
commotion
action
me

this symphony, hear it?
roots
evolving
santosha
can
why not
peace
repose
us

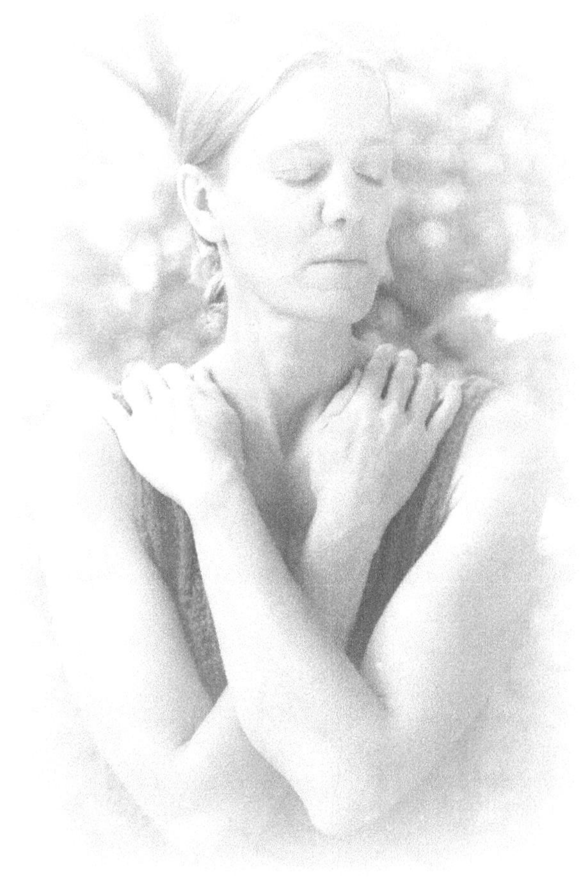

holy smoke

bienvenido a la iglesia del pacto
walk humbly
saturday sidewalk invitations . . .
up steps and through entrances grand greetings
    from tapers, dark timber and stories told in glass
seeking, forever seeking

the trail of that familiar concoction of spices . . .
storax, onchya, galbanum, frankincense
at once transported back to row 8 or 9, stage right, st. mary's
squirming, distracted, ambling through motions
readings, gospels and gifts
hymns, refrains and offers of peace
rituals . . . out of body

but today . . .
formalities absent,
i come drifting back ripened and at ease
pausing solo with just the breath
new permissions seized
take what i will
a suggestion in song #112
"keep awake, be always ready" . . .

of course . . .
show up
wake up
mercy, mercy, mercy
take refuge in the wheel
the essence so familiar

horns and people pulsing outside
"clouds the spirit's light conceal," goes the tune
yet under this roof of some covenant,
the spirit of all seasons is exposed
keep awake, be always ready . . .
a collision of doctrine and years and attention
finally, a circle completes

a sweet fragrance, rising smoke . . .
scripture and dharma, communion and sangha, pulpit and cushion
formulas . . .
symphonies unfolding, an opus they need not be
the poetry reduces

off peak in this house of pews and pipes and tradition
holy, holy, holy

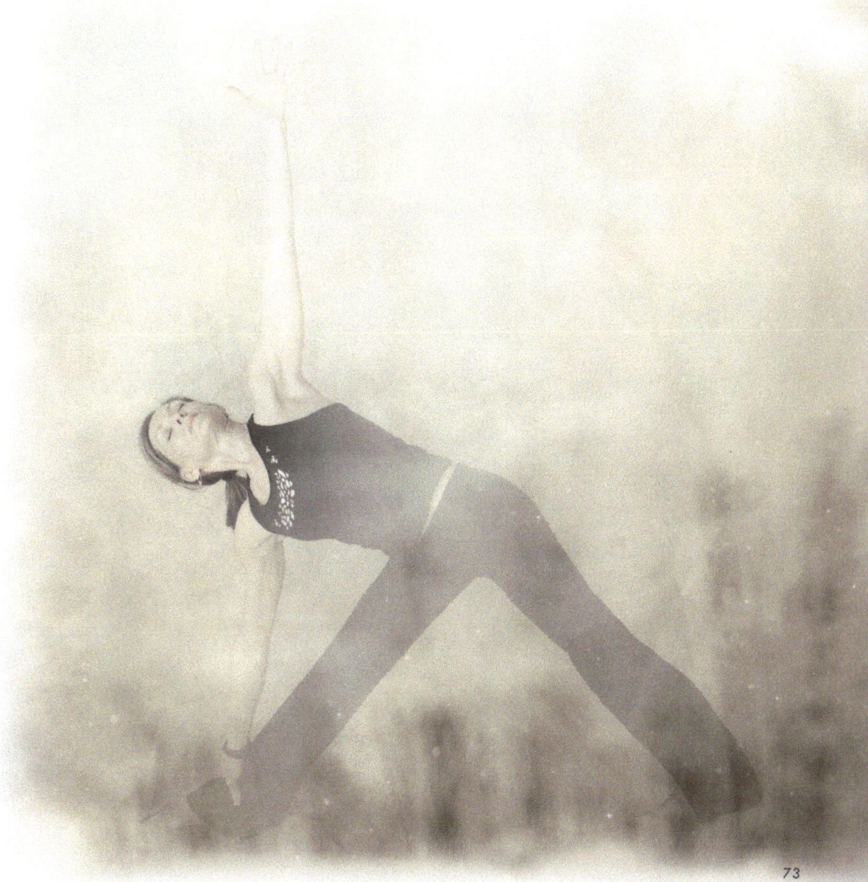

hovering

beings of expansion
beings of contraction
the back and forth

inhale
exhale

awake
dormant

cheer
gloom

fist
shake

tomorrow
never

passionate
prim

of course
no
love
hate

fluid
frozen

yours
mine

hidden
bare

then the poet arrives
loyal to this gospel
decoding what hovers
the scribe

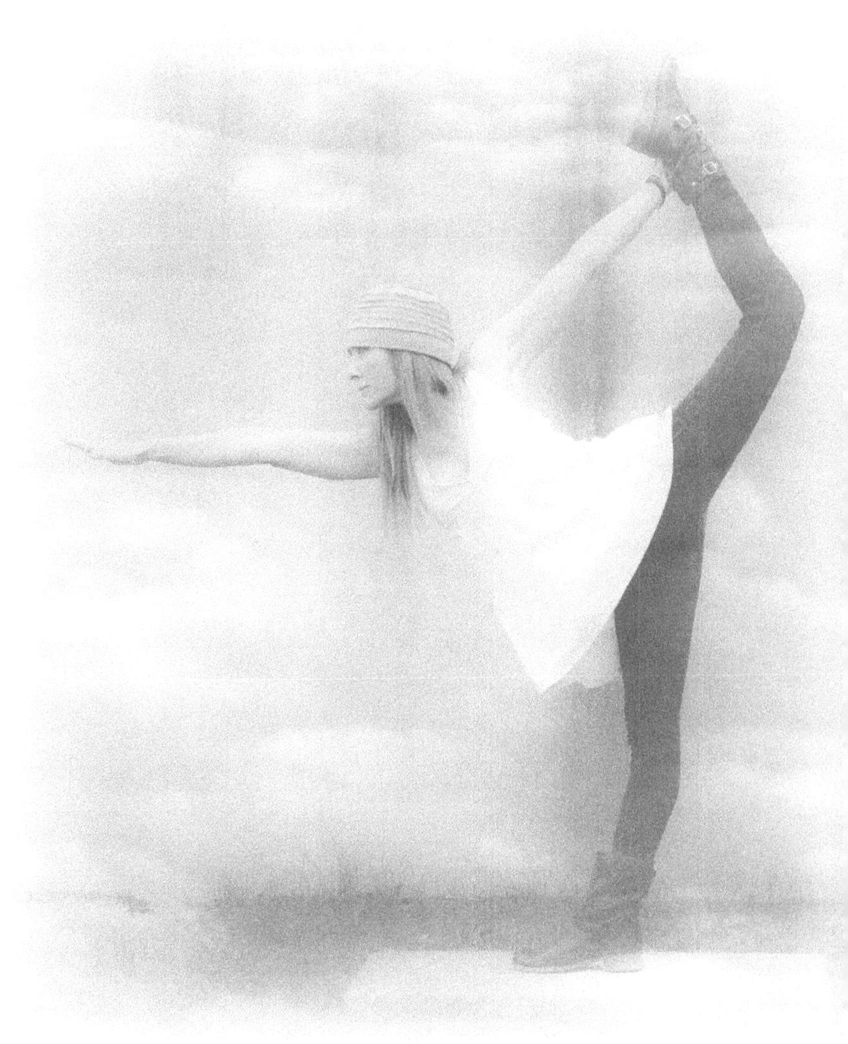

interludes

and, just like that i am reminded of the interludes . . .

inhale, exhale,
sleep, wake,
red, green
open, close
conscious, unconscious
reach, fold
right, left
words, silence
question, answer
fist, peace
thirst, quench
winter, spring
confusion, clarity

the small spaces tucked in between,
infinite opportunities
game changers
the effects rippling . . .

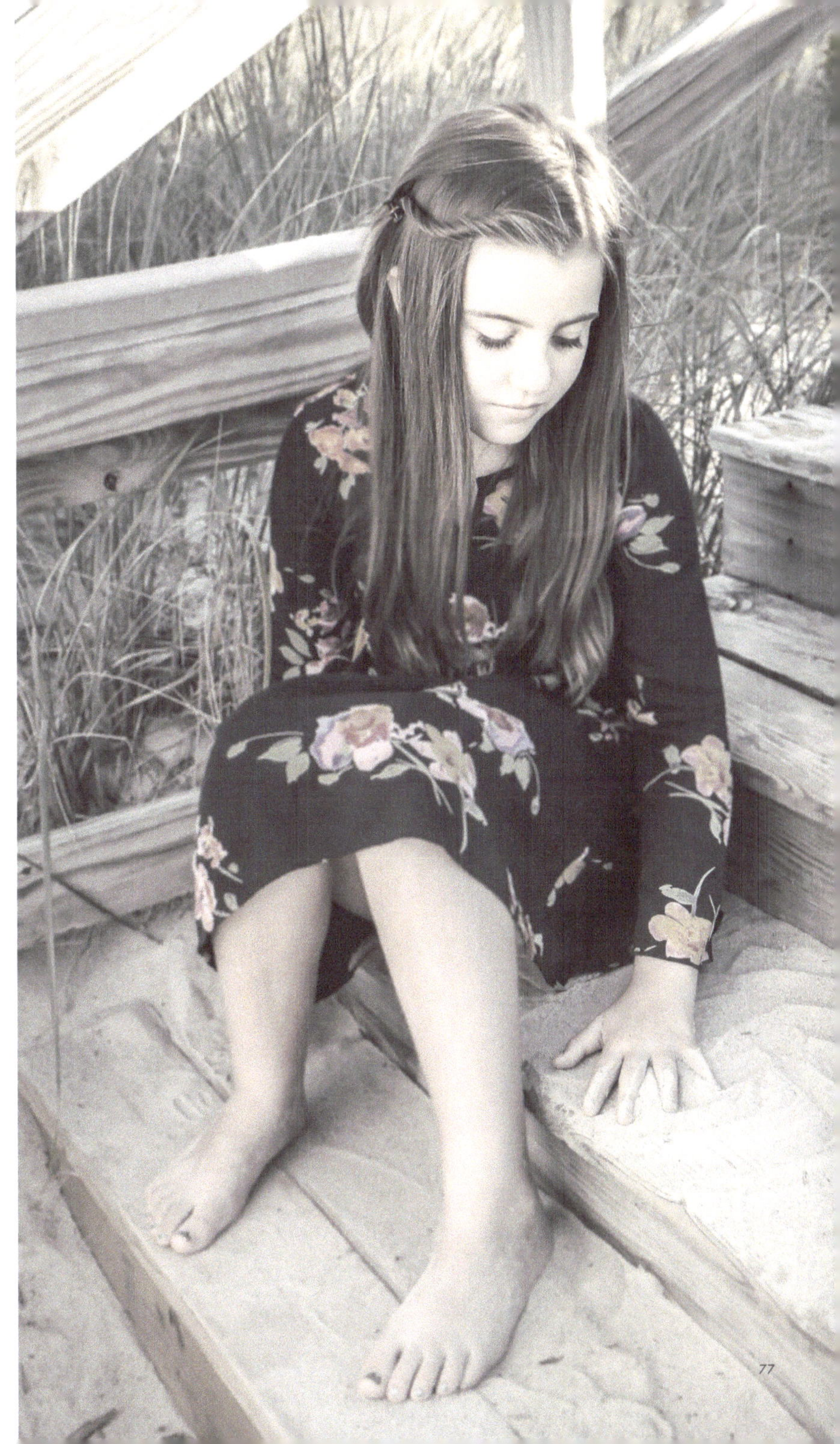

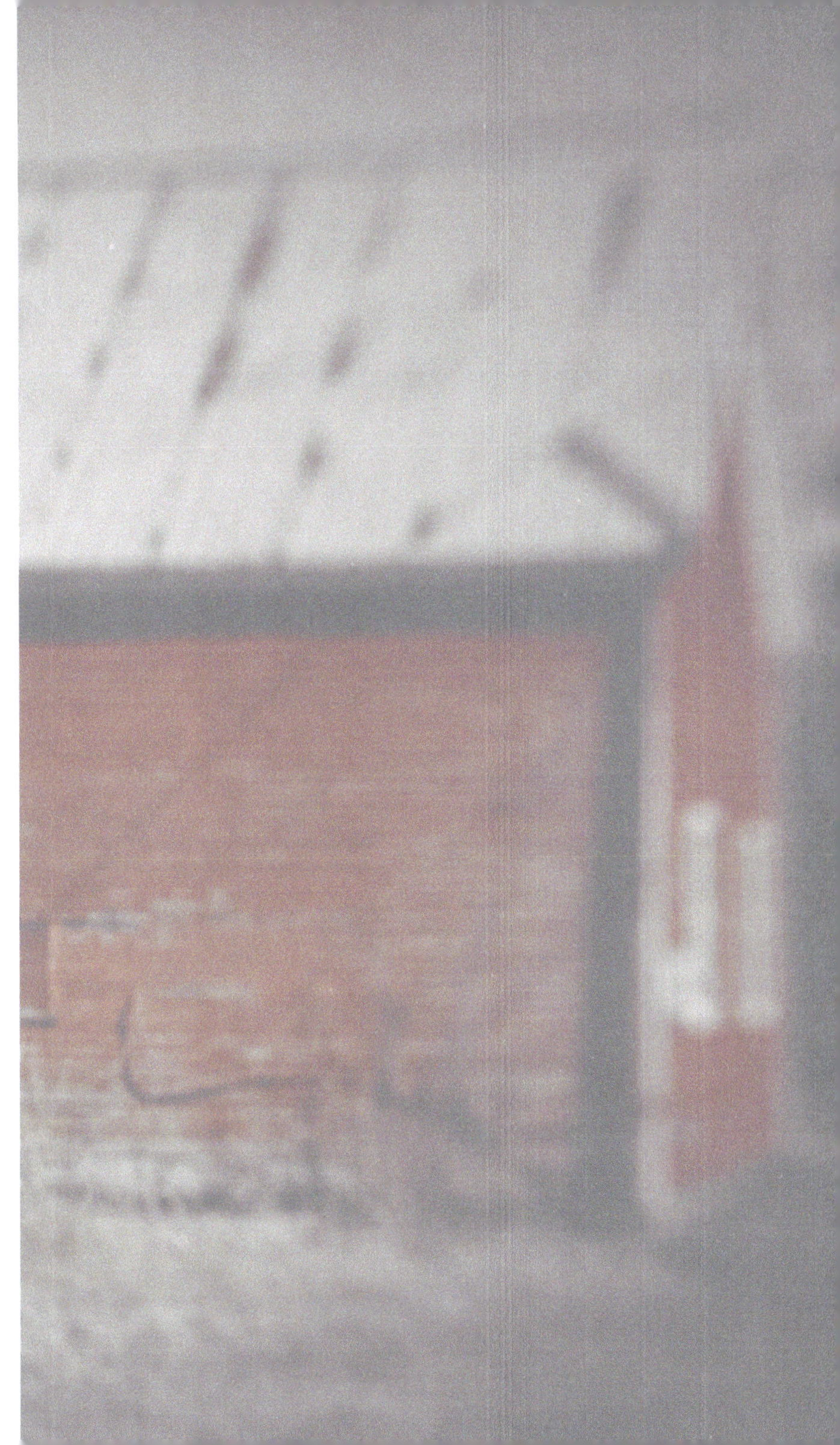

mirror mirror

not the fairest of them all . . . stretch it as you will
ragged limbs, vacant
foundation tattooed
all dusty and mousy
its tomorrows hazy

but above its withering coat, poised, of will
propped by some current of tenacity
guts and spunk and knowledge
weary and worn spending much for each new dawn
yet showing up, ever faithful
perched nobly amongst boyish neighbors of shiny habits . . .
the mighty

towering over the green, quietly preaching grit
concerned for appearances long falling off with each season
paying no mind to the vanity of the fairest
deep rooted and enduring
a sage for the rookies
as if to say follow me

a sage for ME as i study this reflection
examining my place among the budding
years fading, game tapering
still a climbing
a keenness unbounded
unphased by the mellowing

fueled by deep roots and history not mirrors
a sage for ME . . . these branches frazzled

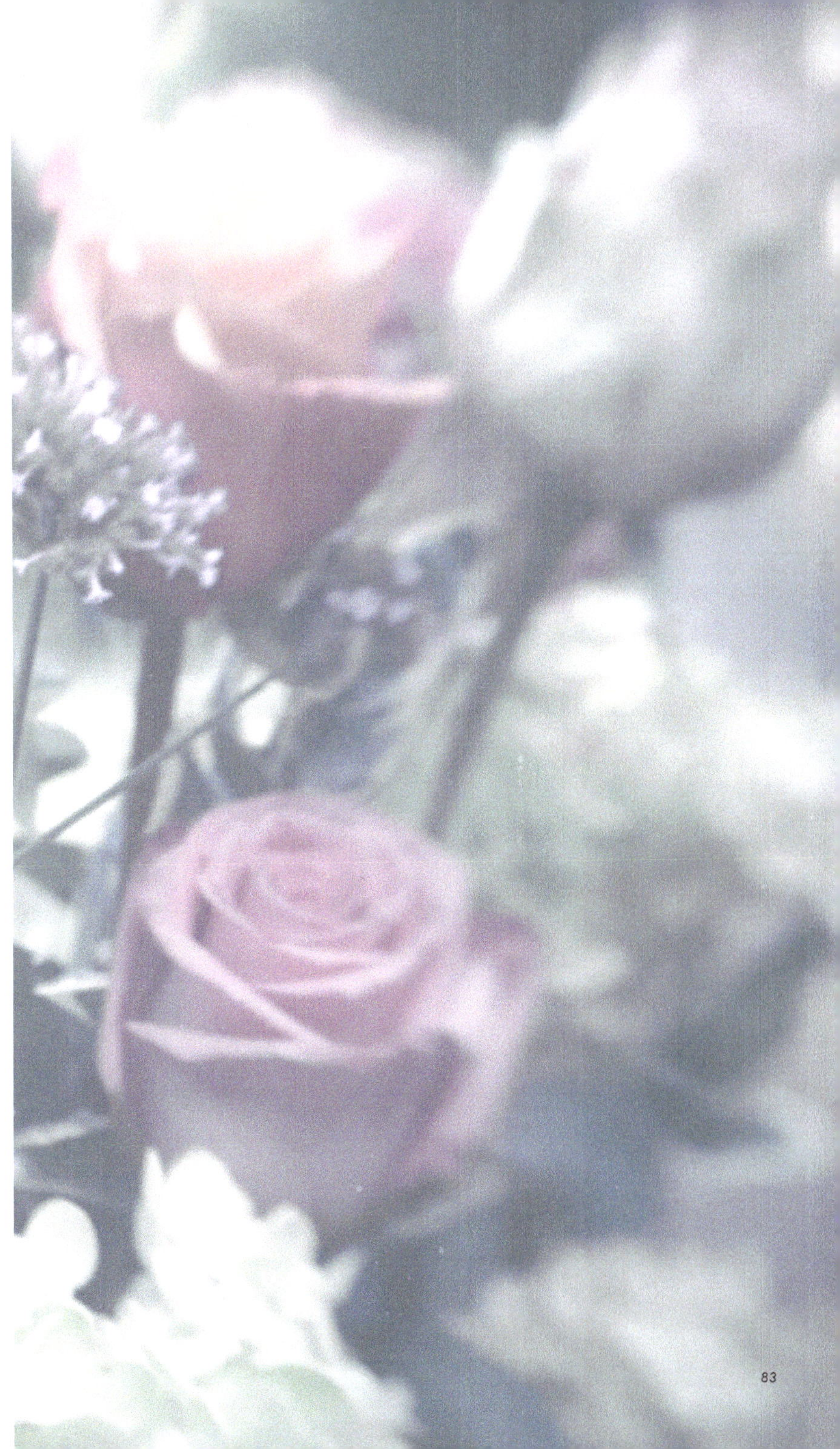

(most likely) to succeed

these flocks swimming above, all current
in pairs, and sometimes not
points north, points west
following their fancy to whatever perch
no apprehension
no invitation
just going

from my sleep they wake me
beating out the sun with their debates
and in the evening from my rest they keep me
clinging to their points
no filter
no pause

at times it's a symphony
stealing bows behind the chatter,
the clutter of these trucks, the day's multi-tasks
their fanfare offered freely
no acknowledgment underfoot
still, caroling

now the afternoon rain has lifted, the day begins its dimming
my pace not so dizzy
eyes drawn up to their flight
to the sky they go, all sonic again
moved by their own spirit
no ticket, no cue, no timed departure
just up, up . . . and

for one second, can i stop all my fixing, all my tuning them out
make room for their case?
can i just wonder what that must feel like
. . . to lift off?
points north, points west
unweighted
recalculated by your own wind
stowing nothing
nothing but your gypsy

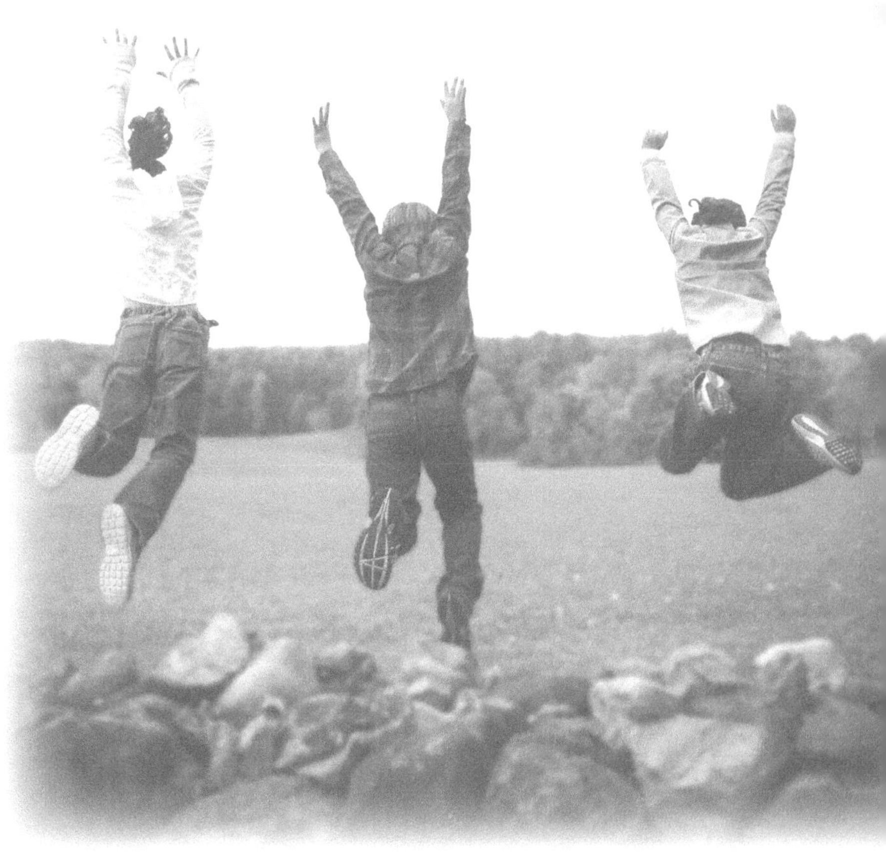

not shrinking . . .

how many times have i skimmed past
on foot, on wheels

the corner of main and lowell
four lanes east and west collide with four north and south
this towering green ash
all history and grandeur

but today it is autumn
perhaps seeing it for the first time
catching every flicker of integrity
being entire

a certain limb at its core
reaches reaches reaching
beyond the margins
#2 on any given october day past sunset
stabbing up at the ether, through the glove's web
insisting

today it is autumn
four days in
all the essential ingredients
my mind in some stage of repose
over horns and machines improving things
wisdom knocks

the compassionate witness towering over the bus stop
not judging the motorists behaving badly
not shrinking from lack of applause
competing against no thing
in absolute communion with what is
imbibing every ounce
falling into the light
yielding

not seeking
just here

just present for the dazzle
this mouthful, fraxinus pennsylvanica
coming back each morning despite the uncertainty
deferring all the credit to the sky and its neighbors
and, preaching all we need to know

gold and rings of diamonds
the sage from jersey with his guitars & poetry & tattoos sings
of searching
searching for his beautiful reward
down empty hallways, going from door to door

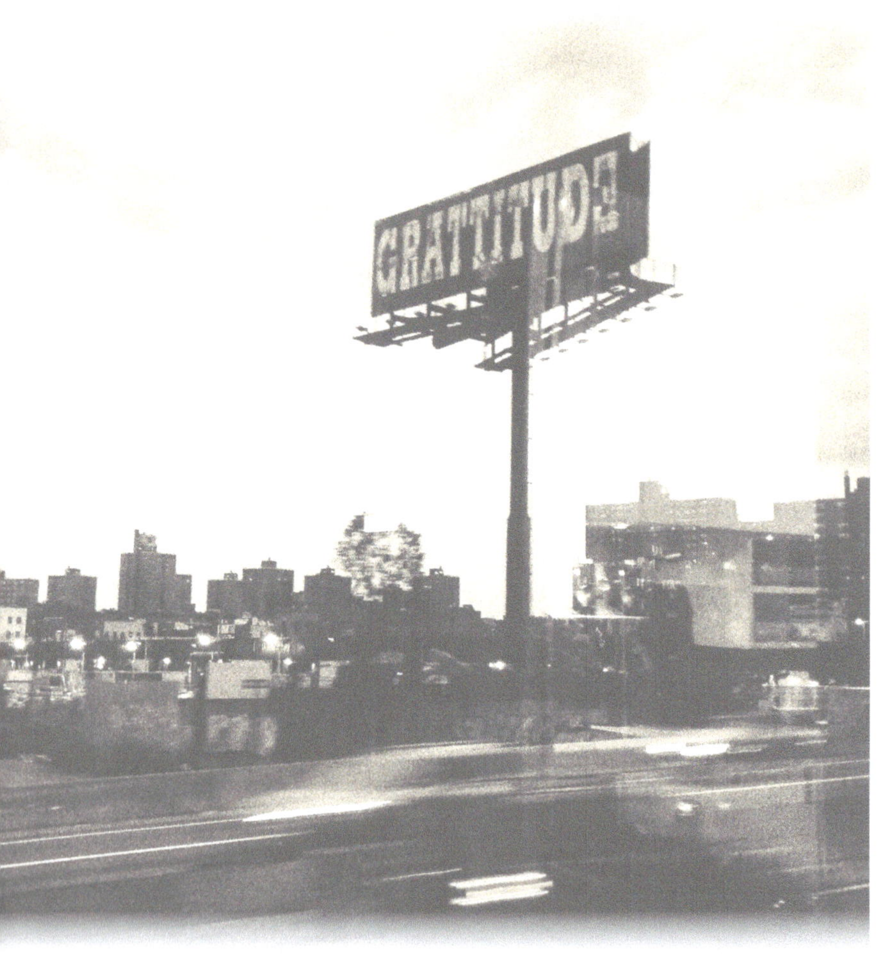
GRATTITUDE

offerings

what i believe is,
we are all at risk
this being human - "a path with no railings"

what i believe is,
the wheel spins, and lands
and, we all mean well

what i believe is,
we forget

what i believe is,
we all have a story
each tale deserving of the same volume

what i believe is,
the orchestra will never be in harmony if we don't
    pick up our instrument

what i believe is,
(some days) the suffering is optional

what i believe is,
these trees, this wind, these merry waters whose rim i roam . . .
have a gospel for us
which is, common sense
nothing to denounce

what i believe is,
the sunshine will prevail

what i believe is,
today's offering . . . this backstage gesture of nothing more
than a lucid moment tallying some blessings and considering
things other than "me"
this somewhere, my start
what i believe is . . . this will echo

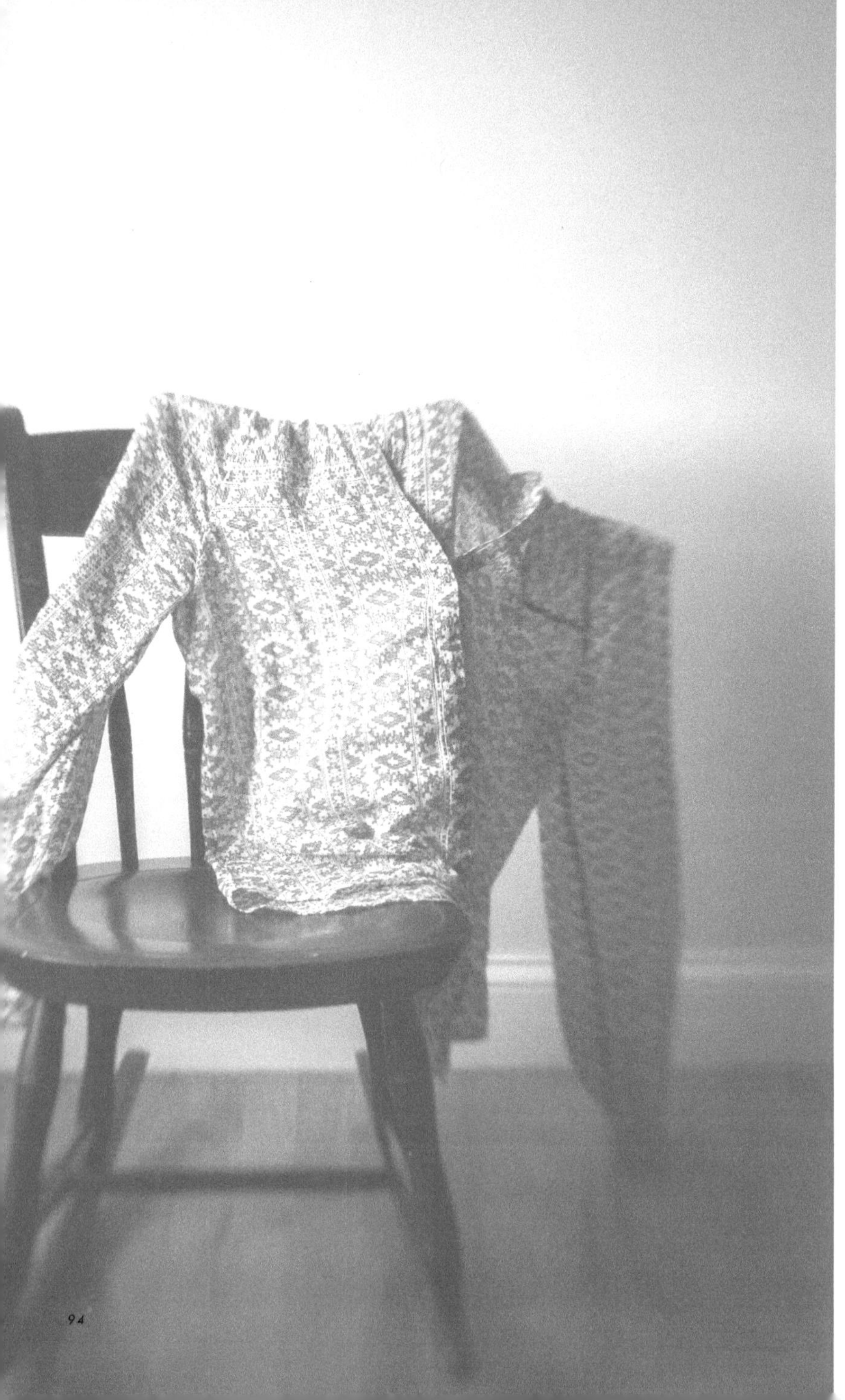

(one) human predicament

life
childhood
wonder
split
sisters

learning higher
live free . . . or
sisters

my number two
labor
new life, joy
cancer
healing

new life again, joy
dementia
honey
sisters
tradition
death
heartbreak
lymphoma
sisters
exhale

stage two/three
terror
recovery
my number two, still

poetry, flutes, frank and vacationland
miracles
turns and twists

cancer . . . again
another bomb
exhale
tomorrow
faith . . .

long way home

this fantasy of perfect visibility,
among demands too many
what if?
what if we clear just *some* of the dust
some of the dust from the eyes

10,000 joys
this world is happening
10,000 sorrows
tousled are we
what if?
what if we (on purpose) lie down under all that

stay versed in the work . . .
the haze, the weight, the swell
and, its human error
its forever call for calibration

consider the water, idling
how it renders scrutiny powerless
curls and sways on its surface can't delete a pool's trying

reasonably clear
reasonably clear
reasonably clear
and then, the exhale

away with just *some* of the debris
best shot . . .

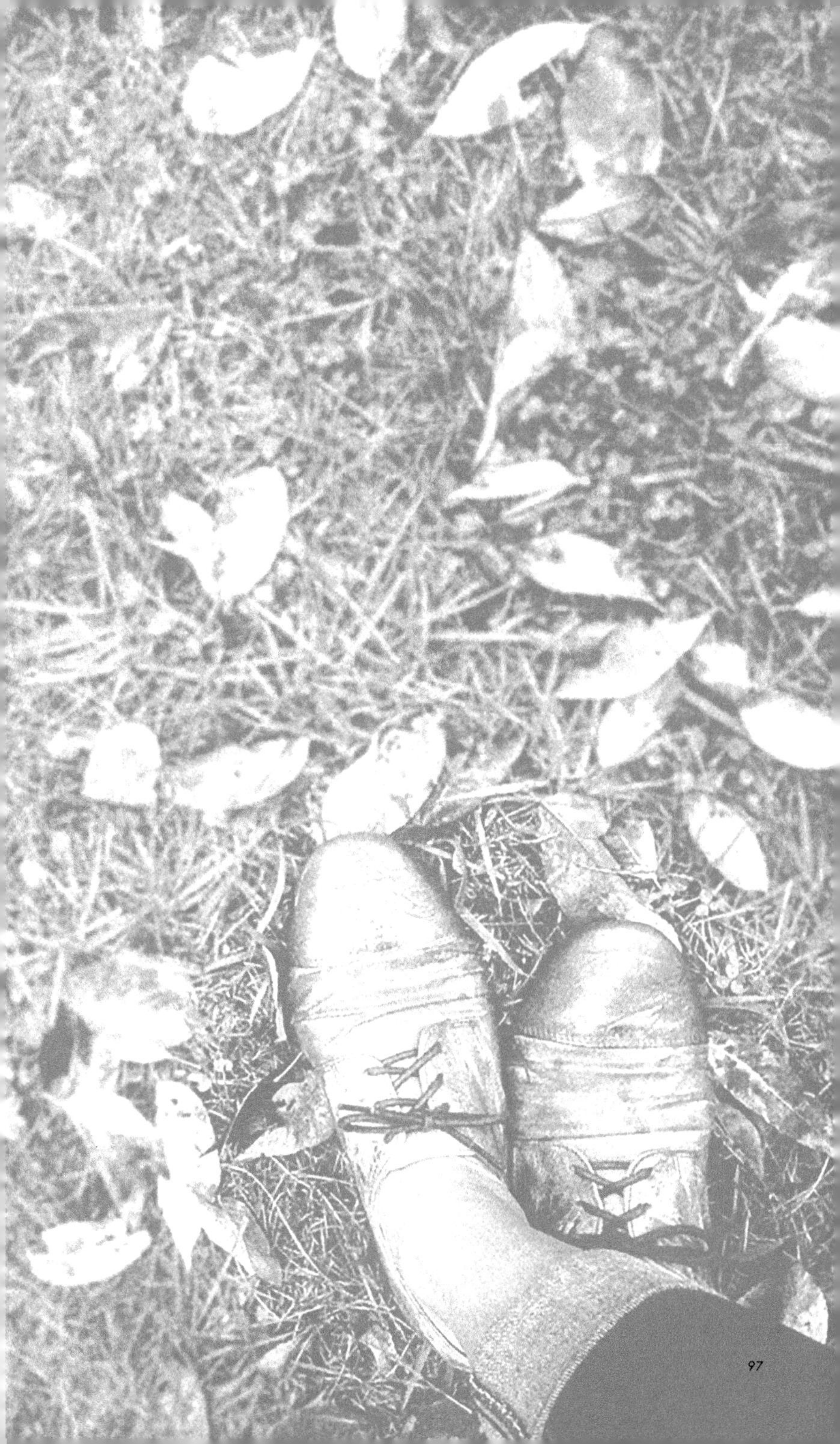

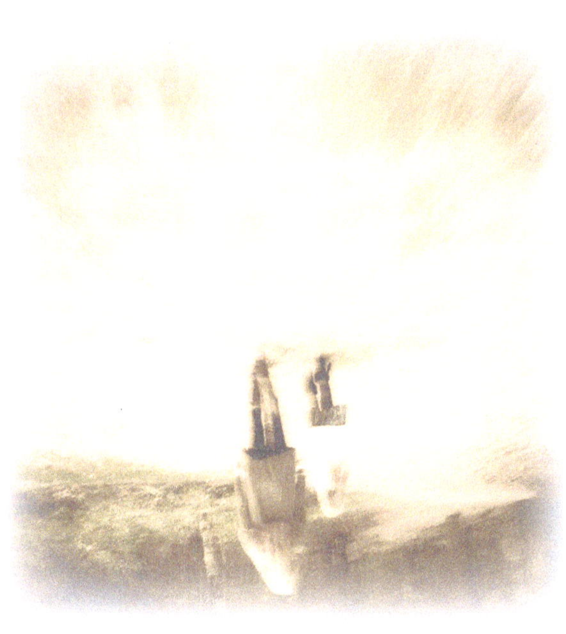

www.ingramcontent.com/pod-product-compliance
Lightning Source LLC
LaVergne TN
LVHW052306100826
845147LV00006B/689